Brand Revolution

Brand Revolution

Rethinking Brand Identity

Marie-Claude Sicard

First published 2013 by
PALGRAVE MACMILLAN

Palgrave Macmillan in the UK is an imprint of Macmillan Publishers Limited, registered in England, company number 785998, of Houndmills, Basingstoke, Hampshire RG21 6XS.

Palgrave Macmillan in the US is a division of St Martin's Press LLC, 175 Fifth Avenue, New York, NY 10010.

Palgrave Macmillan is the global academic imprint of the above companies and has companies and representatives throughout the world.

Palgrave® and Macmillan® are registered trademarks in the United States, the United Kingdom, Europe and other countries.

ISBN 978–1–137–01948–6   hardback

This book is printed on paper suitable for recycling and made from fully managed and sustained forest sources. Logging, pulping and manufacturing processes are expected to conform to the environmental regulations of the country of origin.

A catalogue record for this book is available from the British Library.

A catalog record for this book is available from the Library of Congress.

10   9   8   7   6   5   4   3   2   1
22 21 20 19 18 17 16 15 14 13

Printed and bound in Great Britain by
CPI Antony Rowe, Chippenham and Eastbourne

Only dead fish swim with the stream.

Native American proverb

CONTENTS

LIST OF FIGURES

What's new?

Shakespeare. No, don't run away! I'm going to show you that without reading a single line of the Bard, his work has something to teach us even about a subject as trivial as commercial brands.

In one of those outbursts of emotion that adolescents are wont to mistake for poetry, Juliette declares to Romeo that a rose would smell just as sweet if it had a name other than "rose." Thinking themselves immune to all possible criticism when shielded by such a prestigious name as Shakespeare, generations of cunning folk have repeated this declaration whenever they wanted to affirm that it is the object, and not the name, that counts.

Except that (with all due respect to Shakespeare) it's quite possible that this is false. We see and hear different things according to whether we say *chien*, *dog*, or *perro*. The link between words and things varies according to space and time, as does the meaning of words. And words bear traces of these variations for centuries and sometimes even for millennia after their invention. Europeans, for example, have slightly different relationship to work according to whether they're German, English, Italian, Spanish, or French: the former respect work, whereas the others are wary of it and accord it only a secondary importance. Is this a matter of different mentalities or of different languages—or might the two be related? In Italian, "work" is *lavoro*, from the Latin *labor*, and is associated with the idea of "*fatica*," a painful and prolonged physical or mental effort. In French, *travail* translates as "work," and yet even in common parlance the two words have slightly different resonances: *travail* bears the memory of the Latin *tripalium*, an instrument of torture made of three stakes, while the English language inherited "work" from High German, which borrowed it from a Greek word that simply means an "activity" or an "action." In Northern Europe, the word is neutral. In Southern Europe, less so. Etymology is the buried, unconscious part of language. This must be recognized in order to make out what's hiding behind similarities that are convenient but sometimes deceptive, and that fool us in ways that are always revealing.

So why do we say "brand" on one side of the Atlantic and *marque* on the other? Beneath the apparent equivalence of these two words, might there not be two different conceptions of what a brand is?

A few years ago, the question might have seemed frivolous, but the context has made it a necessary one. Until then, the English-speaking conception of marketing and brands was so dominant that it was adopted without question by professionals the world over. The real debate (or rather controversy) came from elsewhere, from consumers, and grew increasingly lively. It wasn't the first time that brands had been accused of being an unduly intrusive presence in the public sphere, but this time the wave swept the entire world with the success of *No Logo*.[1] The best-selling book galvanized Western readers' latent irritation and earned overwhelming approval from consumers, while the accused, advertisers and ad agencies, proved incapable of mounting the slightest collective defense. Here and there, a few individual responses appeared, but none had the any effect on the disrepute afflicting brands and marketing, which has only worsened in the years since.

Isn't it possible that this disrepute originates in a vision of the marketing trade unconsciously channeled by the word "brand" in a direction the public is no longer willing to follow? And, if this is true, might it not be possible to blaze another trail by exploring the word "*marque*"? What is striking about the French word is precisely the reverse of what the English one connotes: instead of a clear difference between technical language ("brand") and colloquial language ("mark"), in French the word "*marque*" ("mark") does double duty, signifying in normal usage a trace or an imprint left by something or someone, and in its technical usage a material sign or name used to distinguish a manufacturer's products or a seller's merchandise. Why not tease out the implications of this twofold usage? The French language leads us to do so almost naturally, and so instead of keeping commercial "marks" separate from the rest, why not bring them back to their common origin instead? By transferring the idea that a brand is a mark or an imprint to the commercial sphere, new perspectives and tools may appear that make it possible to defuse some of the tensions brought about by English-speaking practices that have reached an impasse.

And so the Fingerprint Method was born, as an operational consequence of more general reflection on the causes that led classical marketing to this impasse.

And for those who raise their eyebrows at the idea of an edifice resting upon such fragile foundations (can just two little words really give rise to so many grand ideas?), don't forget that everyday science lends new credibility to the following poetic insight, beautifully formulated by Tristan Tzara: "We think with our tongues."

Yes, we think with words and images, and not with abstract ideas. It is not our convictions that influence our actions, but first and foremost language, which influences our convictions and thus causes us to act. *Through the Language Glass*, a work which enjoyed surprising success in light of its erudition, offers proof of this.[2] Daniel Kahneman's work on behavioral finance, which earned him the Nobel Prize in Economics in 2002, has also shown this to be so. In collaboration with Amos Tversky, Kahneman studied the cognitive biases at work in stock market turbulence, and in particular elaborated on the theory of framing effects that the Palo Alto Group[3] had been analyzing for decades. Numerous researchers are now following the trail he blazed, including when that trail crosses into marketing territory, and they confirm that words give rise to thoughts.

In other words, the mental image we have of a daffodil is not exactly the same as the one we have of a "*jonquille,*" and the same is true of the words "*marque*" and "brand." If the latter word no longer has the public's support[4] without which it is nothing, the time has come to rethink it.

And at the same time, to rethink another word that has become central in marketing, a word that everybody uses as if each of us knew exactly what it meant: identity. As we will see, the word's meaning hardly goes without saying. It generates much debate, but also a lot of hot air. Where the word "identity" is concerned, the old adage holds true: you reap what you sow. Unless we nourish the word with real meaning, we're bound to harvest a lot of silly received ideas.

* * *

Before being a commercial brand, a brand is thus a mark, a trace left by something or someone, a personality, a landscape, an event. These mental traces are in general all the sharper for being associated with a strong emotion, like fear. I recall how I jumped in the air at the sight of a harmless grass snake as I was walking in the woods one day. Fifteen years have passed since, but the memory of that instant remains as vivid as ever, and I continue to be struck by the fact that although I saw a moving grass snake, the image in my memory is frozen in place, and perfectly sharp and clear. It doesn't resemble the film that unfolded before my eyes but rather an engraving. To deduce from this that this engraving is stored somewhere in my brain's hard drive is the natural next step, but it's one that we mustn't take, as the latest research shows.

Indeed, cognitive science has made great strides in its exploration of human memory. Scientists are close to knowing how the mental traces we call memories are formed. They know that they are scattered among several parts of the brain, and even several parts of the body, and that they are perpetually reworked as time passes. In short, these scientists know how to analyze what happened when I saw the grass snake.

For example, they explain that we all possess a proto-memory, which has been conditioned for hundreds of thousands of years to spot what once constituted the greatest danger for the human species: wild animals, reptiles, spiders, rats, poisonous plants. These unconscious but very real memories slumber in the reptilian brain, which reacts in a split second when one of the images surges forth.

Cognitive science also explains how short-term memory works, how it stores and retrieves memories, and how mental impressions form and dissolve. We now know that these impressions are not frozen in place, and that we never remember anything "forever." A mark left in the memory is not etched there like an inscription in marble. A memory impression, because it is produced by a living organism, is a living thing itself. It evolves, changes over time, with circumstances, even when it seems to remain intact.

The same is true for that very particular category of impressions, or marks, called brands. We can observe this from the start of the Industrial Revolution, which is not to say that brands were born at this time,[5] but rather that it is in the nineteenth century that they begin to proliferate and spread into every aspect of daily life. The naturalist novels of the period bear witness to this transformation, and cinema would soon do the same: no depiction of daily life can exclude them from the landscape any longer. Our childhood memories are linked to certain brands, and this is true of everyone, even the greatest artists. L. B. Upshaw offers us an illustration of the fact in one of the chapters of her book on brand identity, recalling a story that is well known to film buffs:

> *Citizen Kane* explores the life of Charles Foster Kane, a fictional newspaper publisher, multimillionaire, and would-be politician roughly patterned after the larger-than-life William Randolph Hearst. The film traces the efforts of newsmen to understand what the real Kane was all about, and particularly what was meant by his last dying word—"Rosebud." No one ever discovers that Rosebud is the name of a snow sled that Kane loved as a boy [...]. Rosebud represented the last time Charles Foster Kane was truly happy. It was at the core of his identity, but it was buried too deep for anyone to find.[6]

It's obviously a charming fable. But has it occurred to you that Rosebud was . . . a brand?

TAKING ON CLASSICAL MARKETING

For those who remain unaware of the fact, marketing textbooks regularly remind us that the word "brand" comes from "branding," the operation that consists in marking livestock with a red-hot iron. Today, the branding ceremony, which unfolds among dust, cries, smoke, and the acrid smell of burned flesh, is accompanied on big American ranches by fairs whose symbolic significance is all the more obvious given that the practice itself has become superfluous, since all it takes is a badge gently clipped to the animal's ear to distinguish it from its neighbor.

Branding livestock is obviously not an American invention. The practice has existed since Antiquity, notably in the Bible, in which we see shepherds identifying their sheep with marks of different colors. What is specific to the industrial era is a technique that is much more efficient, precise, and brutal—in a word, more aggressive. It is this technique that marketing invokes, and this is no accident. As the zealous offspring of the industrial revolution, it adopts that revolution's ideology of conquest and domination: nature and the world belong to he who seizes them, land, herds, and people included.

Animal branding is the unconscious of classical marketing. Like all unconscious events, it is repressed, denied, forgotten—but it manages to find a way around these defense mechanisms. It maneuvers, compromises, and reappears here and there in the remarks of some professionals who would recoil in dismay if one were to note how beholden they are to a way of thinking that is infinitely more brutal than their allegiance to the virtues of classical marketing would have us believe. And yet their words are there as proof: "Every strategy consists in tattooing the brand in the consumer's mind," said Brandt some years ago. "We have to circle and destroy," said Colgate or Elida Fabergé. One book devoted to forging brand loyalty speaks of a strategy for "harnessing" the client. Another speaks of "holding and restraining."

I have no sympathy for that kind of marketing. I think that it is archaic, on its last legs, harmful, and that it's headed in the wrong direction. It simply isn't possible to want to "tattoo," "harness," "restrain," and "circle and destroy" people and at the same time to enter into communication with them. Because communicating with someone means dialoguing with him or her, exchanging, sharing—and not trying, by hook or by crook, to make them say or do what one wants them to say or do. It means that we must begin by assuming the other's freedom, and not their weakness or surrender. It means accepting differences, and not asking people to act and think like everyone else. It means whatever you like, but not trying to shut people up in pens and brand them like cattle.

"Lots of high-flown rhetoric, right from the start," the marketers will say. What does morality have to do with marketing? Not a thing. That was the message that *Brand Babble*[7] wished to convey, in an argument that could be summed up as follows: "Enough sweet talk, a brand's for making money, and that's that." No question of doing anything but helping sell a few barrels of detergent, or renting a car to someone who needs one, or getting a client back in the same supermarket. We're not interested in the improvement of the human condition, only in the consumer's wallet.

This is all well and good, except that the consumer doesn't exist. "Consumer" is nothing more than the name that marketing has given to the part of us that from time to time buys something—a fleeting role that we usually play without thinking, and rarely for more than a few minutes. But because it is a part of us, it is impossible to say where that role begins and where it ends. It is thus also impossible to address it and it alone, ignoring the larger person. It is this person who transmits information to the consumer: there's no getting around it. There is thus no way of isolating the consumer from the human being as a whole.

It thus follows that the rules of human communication apply in every possible scenario—and a business relationship is neither more nor less than one of those possible scenarios. Morality has no say in the matter, and it is not even (or not only) some sort of humanism that must be evoked to justify revising marketing's views on the question. Instead, this revision must take place in the name of a more scientific approach.

Yes, classical marketing, which is so aggressive and so cocksure, which treats the consumer like a cow to be milked and advertising like a whip, a mere tool, doesn't seem to suspect that the tool in question obeys certain laws, whether it is familiar with them or not, whether it has any control over them or not.

Let us take the first of these laws: one cannot *not* communicate. The consequences of this law are simple: companies and brands cannot remain mute. Even if they say nothing, their silence will be interpreted, and interpreted at their expense, either as a sign of impotence or as a mark of their contempt. An example? In the United States, Starbucks closed all of its cafés on 26 February 2008, forgetting to tell people why. The result was that thousands of frustrated consumers immediately began spreading all sorts of alarmist rumors, never having been informed that it was simply a matter of organizing a national training day for all Starbucks employees.

This rule and its corollary ("Everything is communication") have been available to everyone for the last thirty years, but marketing doesn't use them, or at least not much, and usually without being aware of them. From the marketing perspective, the sole contribution of information theory is the classical diagram: Sender > Message > Receiver. Let us be very clear, this diagram is to communication about what the subject-verb-object distinction is to syntax: the description of a fundamental mechanism, perhaps, but nothing more than a mechanism. It's a diagram conceived for transferring information between two machines (two telephones, as it happens) for the least possible cost and with the least possible loss, such that the information in question, in the form of electric impulses or aerial vibrations, arrives at point B in more or less the same state as it was sent from point A.

The last thing that this diagram is concerned with is the content of the transmitted information, and what the people who exchange it will do with that content. Whether it is a declaration of war or of love, a cooking recipe or the result of an exam—this matters not in the least to the technicians of information. If someone on one end of the line says: "I don't understand what you mean," that isn't their problem: they're just transporters. One doesn't hold it against the electrician when some people use the outlet he has installed to plug in an electric saw rather than a Christmas wreath.

Why, then, does marketing continue to believe that this immemorial diagram is the alpha and the omega of communication, when it makes it possible to solve only those problems relating to the *transmission* of information?

For me, this is a mystery. I observe that many people confuse transmission and communication, and yet it seems to me there isn't any way of confusing learning the alphabet with the ability to write *The Adventures of Tom Sawyer*. There are fascinating things to be said and to know about the alphabet, but we ascribe greater value not to the letters that make it up but to Tom's adventures, which trigger our interest, our emotions, our enthusiasm, and to the memories that we have of those adventures long after having read them.

Communication is what gives—or does not give—meaning to information. By itself, information has no meaning. A bit, a letter, a pixel, a number have no significance without someone to give them one. "Three dead in an airplane accident in Spain" is a piece of information but it has no *a priori* meaning for a Kenyan. And this is why we are bombarded with more and more information, to which we are increasingly indifferent: it's not just egoism or saturation, but that most of this information, for us, has no meaning, isn't linked to our experience, and remains what it is on a piece of newsprint or the television screen: lifeless letters, hollow words, senseless images. In any event, marketing is well aware of this: for several years now, desperately seeking brand content, it's been on a quest for meaning. Might we be so bold as to ask it to stop for a moment, so as to take the time to understand what that means?

MEANING IS BORN OF RELATIONSHIPS

Rather than starting with a theoretical definition, I'll take an example of something which, for me, has no meaning. And too bad if it necessitates a confession that shows me in a slightly unflattering light, since many of my readers, I am sure, have already found the key to the mystery.

The last sequence of *2001: A Space Odyssey* has no meaning in my eyes. I've never understood it. Of course, I've read quite a bit on the subject, but nothing that really clears things up for me, not even the hypothesis that it's a cinematographic acid trip. Whether it's true or not, that doesn't explain the last word of the story for me. I can understand the long tracking shot at the end of *Zabriskie Point*, even if nothing happens for seven minutes in a row. But the images at the end of *2001*, no.

It wasn't until I became interested in communication theory that I started to understand what was preventing me from finding any kind of meaning in that sequence.

Meaning, says communication theory, is born of a relationship. It doesn't exist by itself, hidden in a film or at the heart of a poem or a painting—or in a gesture, an object, a word. It exists from the moment someone establishes a relationship between that gesture, that object, that word, and what surrounds them. To understand the meaning of "hole," for example, there has to be something around the hole: cloth, paper, a wall, clouds. The hole has no meaning except with respect to its environment, and to the observer.

This is a troubling revelation, for we have frequently been taught that the opposite is true, and this is especially so where the teaching of literature, music, and painting is concerned. In *Moby Dick*, for example, doesn't the metaphor of the great whale hunt conceal a hidden meaning, namely the struggle of good against evil or the punishment of sinful pride?

If the author wanted this to be the meaning, it must be there, but that doesn't guarantee that this is the meaning each new reader will find there. And if we can't find this meaning, that means it isn't there, even if the artist wanted it to be. It is undeniable that *Guernica* has a precise meaning intended by Picasso, but if someone looks at the painting without being familiar with the painter's story, or with History, he may see something completely different, or nothing at all, and then the initial meaning disappears or is changed. This is another, disturbing fact of communication theory: what has been understood is what has been communicated.

It is because I link the final sequence of *2001: A Space Odyssey* to nothing—nothing that comes before it in the film, nothing in my personal experience or cultural background—that I don't understand it. It's an object that I can't figure out what to do with: I can't make heads or tails of it. It doesn't speak to me. There is no relationship with anything I know or have known. This implies that the meaning is not in the image but in my head, in the back-and-forth movement between the two, and in the links that I establish among various elements.

Brands are right to ask the question of meaning: the ones that don't have any simply don't exist in the eyes of consumers. Let us take Mrs. Miller, an imaginary customer whom we shall have the pleasure of meeting again in the course of this book. If we place beneath her eyes the names Pataugas and Omas, they won't have any meaning for her. They don't exist, they haven't the slightest value, not even the beginning of an identity. And yet these are well-known brands in France and Italy, but she's never heard of them, she doesn't know if they're people, cities, rivers, varieties of roses, the names of horses, or something else. She links them to nothing.

No identity, no meaning, and vice versa. The question of meaning is thus indeed a central one, and it is directly linked to the question of brand identity. As for knowing exactly what meaning is, we'll see that it's not what is buried in one or another of the brand's components, but what emerges from the relationship of its various components: the relationship among them, on the one hand, and between these components and the consumers on the other. In other words, meaning is not a quality intrinsic to an object or an action. In and of itself, a product doesn't have enough meaning to distinguish it from the category "raincoat," "watch," or "automobile." A brand has the capacity to make the product stand out from the crowd of anonymous objects, on one condition: that it produces meaning, that is to say that in one way or another it establishes a relationship between the object and its surroundings.

A mental impression is formed the moment I recognize such and such a brand, know which one it is and what it makes—in other words, from the moment I have a clear idea of its identity.

Without an identity, no impression, no imprint, no mark. Without an impression, no brand.

What makes up brand identity, given that it is identity that holds the key to the entire system, and especially the power to leave an impression in people's minds?

This is a question that I've been thinking about for the past twenty years…

WHY COMMUNICATION THEORY?

Over time, I felt the need to change my method: I explain why in detail at the beginning of Part II of this book. But the profound reason was the desire to find an approach that expands on and confirms my conviction that brands are systems, and that we must seek to treat them as such, in a global way—and not by slicing them up into little pieces the way the marketing mix does. Systems theory opens up fascinating perspectives, but they are difficult to put to work in a concrete way without drawing my interlocutors into theoretical considerations for which they don't necessarily have the same curiosity or the same taste as I do.

So I shifted my focus in the direction of communication theory. It's a vast domain, and I couldn't study it all. I chose to use (among others) the discoveries of the Palo Alto Group, as well as those of cognitive science.

I didn't follow the two paths that are usually privileged by marketing for tackling what it calls "qualitative" questions: semiology and psychology. Why? First of all, because even if psychology, like sociology and anthropology, has a great deal to say about identity, it doesn't offer an explanation in and of itself. I didn't ignore these other points of view, but I relativized them. In particular, it seems to me that for decades psychology has placed too much emphasis on our interior life, as if everything originated there— starting with our identity, a sort of rare and precious essence buried deep within us that we must seek, cherish, support, and protect at all costs.

The "new communication"[8] has little reverence for this vision—or this error—promoted by traditional psychology. The Palo Alto Group even invented another vision, whose indifference with regard to received ideas is, in my view, its most salient quality. Without being cowed by psychoanalytic terrorism, this vision doesn't concern itself with sounding the depths of the human psyche and takes little interest in the personal history of each individual. From this perspective, the unconscious, the libido, dreams, and childhood trauma are neither objects of worship nor articles of faith. What this perspective offers instead is a pragmatic psychology[9] for which interior life is not in the least bit sacred. It analyzes communication between humans with the help of a simple and original framework, based on the study of human relations, and attempts to resolve the difficulties of communication through the technique of "brief therapy," which is still practiced today at the famous Mental Research Institute.

As for semiology, the use to which marketing puts it certainly distort its specific value and objectives, but even when it is skillfully used, it usually comes into play later in the process of analyzing brands. It's a precious but fragile auxiliary tool that is delicate to handle because it is closely dependent on the quality of those who use it and still more on their pedagogical talents. Its chief flaw? Being perpetually stuck on the "close-up" setting. This is in fact a limitation rather than a flaw—one comes up against the same limitation when using a microscope, which we can hardly blame for seeing only what it manages to enlarge. But this limitation prevents semiology from seeing the big picture that strategic thinking demands—and this is why semiology, or semiotics, is rarely summoned by the board of directors when it comes time to make a crucial decision. With some rare exceptions, semiologists play a very limited role in building brand identity—or, to be more precise, it sometimes happens that they join in the process of thinking about visual identity, but brand identity cannot be reduced to visual identity alone. Above all, by spending hours with their magnifying glasses deciphering all kinds of objects, texts, and advertisements, semiologists make it seem as though objects and texts always have a hidden meaning whose revelation is sufficient in itself. As I've already said, this is not the Palo Alto Group's point of view. And so, neither psychology nor semiology here, except in very small doses.

Besides, the former has nothing but the most farfetched explanations for the way the grass snake made me jump in the air. And semiology has no explanation at all. But neuroscience makes it possible for me to understand it, and it also makes it possible for me to know a little more than I did twenty or thirty years ago about the way the human mind receives or does not receive an impression from something.

Neurology makes it possible to explain, in biological terms, such phenomena as the feeling of self that undergirds personality and identity or the way mental images are formed. The subtitle of one of Antonio Damasio's books,[10] *Body and Emotion in the Making of Consciousness*, sums up what's essential in three words: the feeling of self involves at once the body, the emotions, and consciousness. Consciousness is nothing without feeling, and feeling is inseparable from the body. Identity takes all three: it is not a pure abstraction, an immaterial principle, an essence.

And yet brand identity is often described in these terms.

Observing the growing gap between what cognitive science has recently taught us about the notion of identity and the way marketing speaks about brand identity, I organized this book in two parts:

- The first part is devoted to giving a summary of everything that has been said over the last few years about brand identity:

  ○ How can we explain the success of an idea that is very hard to define and that generates lots of misunderstandings? (Chapter 1)

  ○ Why must we get rid of our preconceived ideas about brand identity (Chapter 2)

  ○ How can we come up with new ways of thinking about brand identity, and in what direction should we take these new ways of thinking (Chapter 3)

- The second part draws operational conclusions from this discussion (Chapter 4) and offers a new method for analyzing brand identity: the Fingerprint Method (Chapter 5).

This new approach takes as its starting point the principle that a brand is a system, and that only a global approach can account for the functioning of this system. As a result, this new approach is based on a necessarily provisional synthesis of what we know, to date, about the logic of communication, which I would summarize in the following way:

- Brands leave impressions, traces, imprints, and marks on us—or else they're not brands.

- These impressions are not due to the brand's "image," to its "territory," or to its "position," but to something deeper and more global: its identity.

- A brand identity is unique: it therefore leaves an imprint that resembles no other, much like a human fingerprint.

- The outline of this fingerprint is inscribed, more or less deeply and regularly, within a figure that has seven poles, each pole corresponding to one of seven contexts that contemporary communication theory tells us we cannot ignore.

- This figure has no center, no core, and each of the seven poles is just as important as the other six, neither more nor less.

- Brand identity includes but goes well beyond visual identity, to which it cannot be reduced.

- Brand identity is not a state, it's an evolving process.

- It is not immaterial, stable, and invariable. It is both material and immaterial, stable in the short term, but not in the middle or long term, and it is variable in all seven of its dimensions.

The path most frequently taken by the brand within the seven-poled figure is its fingerprint: both its trace, and the trace of its identity.

PART I

Brand Identity: A Short History

CHAPTER 1

A Paradoxical Success Story

Every use of the notion of identity begins with a critique of that notion, as Claude Lévi-Strauss used to say. The same holds true for brand identity: the idea lacks reliability because nobody has ever carefully scrutinized its origins and contours. So let's begin by getting rid of the unnecessary baggage that weighs the concept down: prejudices, illusions, and misunderstandings.

A FUZZY CONCEPT FROM THE START

One of my Italian friends, Ennio Borsieri, used to enjoy telling about a famous debate that took place on French television in the 1970s on the theme "Does God Exist?" The debaters were to be a priest and an atheist, both very well known, and everyone was awaiting the confrontation with great interest. But no sooner had the first made his opening argument than the second responded: "What exactly do you mean when you say 'God'?" Even after two hours of discussion they couldn't agree on a basic definition, and so the debate never took place.

At the infinitely more modest scale with which we are concerned here, we could easily fall into the same trap if someone decided to ask: but what exactly do we mean when we speak about brand identity? Marketing thus takes great pains to avoid asking such a question. Remaining faithful to the pragmatist tradition inherited from William James, marketing notes that the concept of brand identity is tremendously useful, and thus uses it, without any unnecessary "soul-searching."

Pragmatism is not only a quality that marketing likes to boast of possessing, At the beginning of the twentieth century, it was the first great current of American thought. In Europe, it has relatively little influence, the intelligentsia having deemed it "philosophy for laymen." It's not clear to me why a philosophy for laymen should be considered any less respectable than another, and in any event it often has the merit of being clearer. But whatever its origins, every philosophy must have a minimum of intellectual rigor. And rigor (not soul-searching) means knowing the meaning of the words one uses.

Nobody really knows what identity is.

Several categories of theoreticians (mainly philosophers, sociologists, psychologists, and anthropologists) have looked into the question, and have been doing so for a very long time, without managing to settle on even a partial answer.

Philosophers were the first to address it, and after twenty-five centuries of effort, they admit that they are helpless: according to them, it's impossible to say what identity is. There have been no lack of attempts, but from Aristotle to Hegel by way of Locke and Hume the question has been raised a thousand times, and with it a dust cloud of ideas that remains hanging in the air, so that we don't really have a clearer view of the matter than we did in the century of Pericles. Indeed, the closer we get to the modern period, the more hesitant philosophers become to tackle the issue. Nietzsche's famous "What does it matter who I am?" is echoed a century later by Michel Foucault: "Don't ask me who I am, and don't tell me that I must remain the same, that's a bureaucrat's mentality." As a historian, Foucault was in a good position to know that identity, in the legal sense of the word, is a recent concern of Western societies, one that is closely related to the growing need for watching over and controlling populations. Many societies didn't attach, or still don't attach, the same importance to this concept as the West does.

As for the sociologists, they are divided on the question of identity. They hesitate to grant it the status of a concept in the strict sense, observe it with a certain wariness, disagree about what the word actually means, and even end up suspecting that it's simply all of the talk about identity that ends up lending a possibly illusory substance to an otherwise elusive and fleeting reality.

Nobody could be clearer in this regard than Zygmunt Bauman, for whom identity is an irremediably ambiguous idea, one that is always subject to controversy, and whose meaning has been swept away in the shifting tides of what he calls liquid societies. It's impossible to give identity a stable, fixed meaning. He writes that in a world where we are witnessing "the accelerating liquefaction of social frameworks and institutions," we must remember that "'fluids' are so called because they cannot keep their shape for long." As a result, "frames, when they are available, should not be expected to last for long." In such a context, "a cohesive, firmly riveted and solidly constructed identity would be a burden, a constraint, a limitation to the freedom to choose, a recipe for inflexibility." He concludes that "the frailty and the forever status of identity can no longer be concealed. The secret is out."[1]

Claude Lévi-Strauss arrives at just about the same conclusion:

With regards to our civilization and the current state of knowledge in varied disciplines—mathematics, biology, linguistics, psychology, philosophy, etc.—it has been observed that the content of the notion of identity is in doubt, and is sometimes even the object of very severe critiques.[2]

This acknowledgment of failure in no way prevents the following from being so:

- We, Westerners of the third millennium, all believe for the moment in the existence of something that we call identity, and to which we attach tremendous importance;

- We think that we have a certain amount of knowledge about how to recognize this identity, about its makeup, and about how it works.

What seems to go without saying for marketing is thus far from being obvious to researchers in the human sciences, and it follows that when we speak about brand *identity*, we're on rather shaky ground. Add to this the fact that the various definitions of *brand* can be quite murky and we end up with a concept, *brand identity*, that is much less clear than it seemed at first glance, since neither of the two words it brings together has a perfectly clear meaning.

HOW SHOULD WE DEAL WITH SUCH A COMPLEX IDEA?

Marketing doesn't like complexity, and seeks by any means possible to pretend it doesn't exist, or to boil it down to something simpler. Brand identity offers the perfect opportunity for such reduction, because from the very first it looks like a concept that is too rich to be directly exploitable. As L. Upshaw notes, a brand isn't just a name, a logo, or some other symbol, but also the employee who rents you a car at the Avis counter, an overnight delivery truck, or the voice of a spokesperson endorsing a car brand like Ford or Chrysler. It's the price of a product at Wal-Mart or Costco, a special feature like Clorox's anti-spill bottle, a warranty, and many other things besides.[3] It wouldn't be hard to find German (or Brazilian, or Japanese) equivalents of these American examples, because whatever is even remotely involved in the brand is part of its identity.

But here we come up against a serious problem: the reductionist temptation. So many elements go into making up brand identity that many professionals, feeling overwhelmed by it all, go about things in the same way: they choose a little piece of the brand continent, outline an area that they know they can deal with, and put up a sign: "Here lies brand identity."

For some, all identity lies in the brand's name. For others, it resides entirely in the product. For still others, it is in visual identity, and nowhere else. Or in the advertising image, or in the distribution network, or in the consumer's mind. When you add to this the fact that each of these approaches correspond to businesses that are frequently in competition with one another (design, innovation, advertising agencies, merchandizing, name-creation consultancies, etc.) and you get some idea of the chaos into which managers are plunged whenever they try to figure out who holds the key to brand identity. It's a new version of the blind men and the elephant: "I've got it!" cries the one who's grabbed it by the tail. "No, it's mine!" cries the one who has it by the ears. "Not at all, it's mine!" says the one who has its trunk. Brand identity is thus pulled in all directions by those who've only grasped part of what it is, for lack of a global view.

We thus find ourselves in a paradoxical situation: an entire discipline discusses and manipulates a concept that nobody can pin down. On the one hand, declarations and testimony abound regarding the importance of brand identity and its complexity, and on the other, definitions are lacking or else are so expansive that they lack sharp contours.

How should such a contradiction be interpreted?

By the fact that, at a given moment, marketing needed a concept like brand identity, just as it needed concepts like territory, positioning, target audience, brand image, and just as it will come up with more concepts in the future. Brand identity is a discovery—or an invention—of Western marketing at the turn of the millennium. Nobody talked about it before, and there's no guarantee that we'll still be talking about it twenty or thirty years from now. But here and now, the concept seems indispensable, and undeniably real.

In fact, brands do indeed seem to possess something like an identity. Clarins doesn't resemble Lancôme, or Estée Lauder, Shiseido, or Clinique, and at the same time, Clarins continues to resemble Clarins. But what, then, is its identity? That which distinguishes it from other cosmetics brands? That which makes it stay the same year after year?

Both, and at the same time. Before going any further, let's keep the following first principle in mind: even if we can't really define identity, we know at least one thing, which is that it is based entirely on the dialectic of same and different. It can only be grasped with the help of complex thinking, the kind that accepts the fact that something and its opposite can be true *at the same time*: change and stability, resemblance and difference, longevity and brevity.

Let us then boldly contradict H. Maucher, the eminently respectable president of Nestlé: contrary to what the subtitle of his book[4] would have us believe, there is no such thing as simple principles for leadership in a complex world. If the world is complex—and who would claim that it isn't?—then we must accept it as it is, instead of trying to force it into the straitjacket of what is erroneously referred to as "Cartesian" logic. Even the most serious journals are now trying to encourage companies to benefit from complexity rather than struggling against it in vain.[5]

Moreover, brand identity is a good example of the contradictions we must face, whether we like it or not, because we cannot avoid the disconcerting observation that in this case marketing is using a concept that the specialists all deem indefinable, elusive, and unstable.

Is it then the case that the beautiful constructs that some brands create on the basis of their identity are actually founded on quicksand?

IN SEARCH OF A BIRTH DATE

It's not easy to determine when the notion of brand identity emerged, but we can be sure of at least two things:

- Its emergence is recent;

- It was immediately adopted.

This in itself is an unusual phenomenon. Without any pretense of being exhaustive, a rapid survey of the literature on brands shows that the notion of identity emerged and was fully developed over the course of the 1990s. It is thus barely more than twenty years old. That isn't much, when you consider that most of the big industrial brands date from the end of the nineteenth century or the first third of the twentieth. What this boils down to is that for most of their history, brands functioned, and functioned well, without any need of a concept like identity.

So why do we need such a concept today?

At first glance, because the environment has changed, because consumers have changed, because the rules of the economic game have changed, and because markets have grown to encompass the entire planet. There is no point in describing the causes and consequences of these changes in detail: they are now common knowledge. This only makes it all the clearer that the emergence of brand identity is linked to all of these upheavals.

And yet, marketing doesn't speak of the circumstances surrounding this birth. Generally speaking, history—including its own history—hardly interests it. The most popular marketing textbooks, for example, jump right into the subject without offering any historical perspective. It would be wrong to blame them for this: after all, they're textbooks, and textbooks are works with a practical purpose. A guitar manual doesn't go all the way back to Indian music to explain to beginners how to strum a few chords. But let us take a book that is presented as being "extremely comprehensive," which numbers almost 400 pages, and was authored by top specialists.[6] Each of these specialists examines various concepts and methods, yet none of them is interested in their history.

This absence of any historical approach makes it difficult to know where, when, and why notions such as territory, image, market segmentation, positioning, and brand identity emerged.

What's the big deal, you ask?

The big deal is that marketing cannot presume to be a science if it continues to refuse to take its own genesis into account. And yet it does presume. This presumption is obvious from the titles of certain publications: *The 22 Immutable Laws of Marketing*,[7] *The 22 Immutable Laws of Branding*,[8] *Gravitational Marketing: the Science of Attracting Customers*.[9] And we have known about it since the first debates in the 1970, which raised the question of marketing as a science[10]—a question that has never been answered. Why? Because there can be no science without a critical examination of the foundations of that science, in other words without epistemology. And there can be no science either without some theoretical reflection. Marketing is as averse to the one as it is to the other.

TWO EVASIVE MANEUVERS FOR AVOIDING THE QUESTION OF ORIGINS

To compensate for this double blind spot, two insidious and usually unconscious errors have sunk their claws into marketing, especially when it is a question of dealing with so-called qualitative concepts like brand identity:

■ The Epiphanic Tendency, which completely does away with history;

■ The Evolutionist Tendency, which uses history for ideological purposes.

Let me explain. *Epiphaneia* means "appearance" in ancient Greek. Epiphany is the appearance of Christ to Paul on the road to Damascus, or the appearance of the Virgin Mary at Lourdes or Fatima. An invisible being suddenly makes an appearance, and nobody knows where he (or she) comes from, indeed nobody even bothers to ask the question. He's there, and that's all that counts.

Every time an author or a marketing manual states point-blank that brand territory, or market segmentation, or any other concept, is this or that, and then talks about the way that concept works, we're in the presence of the Epiphanic Tendency. What's the advantage of going about things this way? The concept in question acquires a self-evident strength such that all questions become pointless, not to say sacrilegious. See what happens if you try to ask out loud about whether, for example, the concept of market positioning is valid, and you'll understand the kind of dead ends to which the Epiphanic Tendency can lead: it nips any sort of discussion in the bud.

As for the Evolutionist Tendency (which borrows from the theory of evolution), it is no less powerful. Marketing, the strong-arm man of economics, could hardly help falling for it, once economics itself borrowed from evolutionary theory in order to understand social transformations, as was (and remains) the case for evolutionist economics.[11] Marketers, too, adore Darwin.[12] It seems to them that a theory based on "the preservation of favorable individual differences and variations, and the destruction of those which are injurious"[13] explains and even fully legitimizes the game of competition. But above all, they enthusiastically embrace the idea of a long evolution over the course of which the "fittest" win out over all the rest, such that each new era, each new species represents an improvement over the one before: the bronze age in comparison to the stone age, animal domestication and farming in comparison to hunting and gathering, mammals in comparison to reptiles, human beings in comparison to monkeys, and Pampers HyperSuperNew in comparison to their predecessors.

The consequences of this universal prejudice are at work throughout the history of marketing: they lead people to believe and to assert that what comes *after* is always *better* than what comes before (hence the popularity of the adjective "new"). In this way, each time that an author or a marketing textbook presents a concept as a form of *progress* with respect to the one that preceded it, whose weaknesses are enumerated, that author or textbook gives in to the Evolutionist Tendency. The phenomenon is particularly obvious where brand identity is concerned, when brand identity is presented as the answer to (or as a form of progress with respect to) the inadequacies of brand *image*.

And it is true that, chronologically speaking, the latter comes before the former. Brand image was born in 1955, in an article in the *Harvard Business Review*, or perhaps even much earlier.[14] As for brand identity, its biography is very blurry – we'll come back to this later – but it seems to date from the end of the twentieth century. So it is almost certain that brand image came along before brand identity.

But what do we read from the pen of one of the most respected authors on the subject? That brand image, the supreme divinity of marketing for almost thirty years, is in the final analysis neither more nor less than…a trap!

> In the brand image trap … the patience, resources, or expertise to go beyond the brand image is lacking, and the brand image *becomes* the brand identity rather than just one input to be considered […]. While brand image is usually passive and looks to the past, brand identity should be active and look to the future […]. While brand image tends to be tactical, brand identity should be strategic.[15]

The same is true in France,[16] where the emergence of the brand identity concept is explained by the flaws in not one but two of marketing's tutelary divinities:

- Positioning, which "asphyxiates the brand's richness of meaning";

- Brand image, because "the obsession with image results in privileging appearance over reality."

Of course, it is perfectly laudable and even necessary to seek to perfect marketing's analytic tools. What is of debatable merit is the tendency to point out the ills of the cause one was defending the day before, on the pretext that because it comes after, the new cause is necessarily superior. I called this tendency the Evolutionist Error, and not the Darwinist Error, because Charles Darwin never speaks of progress, nor even of evolution. Here's why:

> In fact, *evolution* entered our language as the favored word for what Darwin called "descent with modification" because most Victorian thinkers equated such biological change with progress—and the word *evolution*, propelled into biology by the advocacy of Herbert Spencer, meant progress (literally "unfolding") in the English vernacular. Darwin initially resisted the word because his theory embodied no notion of general advance as a predictable consequence of any mechanism of change. […] He never liked *evolution*, and only acquiesced because Spencer's term had gained general currency.[17]

Since I'm not a Victorian thinker, I have no reason to make sacrifices to the myth of progress, nor to believe that each novelty brings the human species one step closer to perfection. The same holds true for ideas: their history does not necessarily reflect improvement. Ideas can come in succession without canceling out or correcting one another. Concepts can come in succession without damaging one another, and in marketing this is especially so, because it's not an exact science. Or, to put it differently: novelty is a fact, not a sign of quality.

A SWIFT AND RECENT EMERGENCE

For lack of an exhaustive inquiry into everything that has been said and written about marketing since its origins, it is impossible to assign a precise date and birthplace to the notion of brand identity, nor is it possible to determine its parent or parents with any degree of certainty.

But we can affirm all the same, and without great risk of error, that the notion was truly developed in the last decades of the twentieth century. A good clue is offered by D. A. Aaker, one of the most well-known marketing professors and consultants on the subject. Two of his books can serve as reference points:

- In the first, *Managing Brand Equity*,[18] the back cover jacket provides a general overview of the work that divides "brand capital" into five parts, the fourth of which is devoted to "brand image." The notion of brand identity is nowhere to be found.

- In the second, *Building Strong Brands*,[19] the same principle is at work: on the back cover, a summary in three parts of unequal importance. The second, in the middle, is by far the one that takes up the most space. It is titled "Brand Identity System." The third part is titled "Brand Identity Implementation System."

The two books were published five years apart. In this brief span of time, the notion of identity emerged with such strength that it takes up almost all of the space devoted by the author to the art of "building strong brands." Where did it come from? It's a mystery. How did the author come to develop this concept? Neither the introduction nor the text itself provide an answer. The author defines brand identity as the sum of twelve components, grouped into four chapters. What is the basis for this classification? This is never specified. The author's authority prevails. And then there was brand identity. Are we by chance dealing with a phenomenon of spontaneous generation? No, but what we *are* dealing with is the Epiphanic Tendency.

The same is true for another author and another book: *Building Brand Identity*,[20] published in 1995. The Preface states immediately that when a brand is threatened, "it's best defense is a formidable brand identity," and goes on to explore the question of how one goes about building that identity. What experiences, what reflections led the author to this conclusion, which is also a point of departure? Impossible to say. That doesn't prevent the book from providing interesting analyses that I will have occasion to cite several times, but the genesis of the concept remains unknown.

As for the histories of marketing that have appeared recently, in R. S. Tedlow's book[21] brand identity is mentioned briefly two or three times as an essential element in Coca-Cola's success, and in F. Cochoy's book[22] it doesn't appear at all. In any event, neither work is focused on the history of concepts used in marketing.

I therefore have no choice but to venture a few hypotheses.

There's no point lingering over the first, which links the emergence of identity to the wearing down of the brand image concept—this hypothesis seems quite plausible.

It would be equally pointless to offer any commentary on the second, which focuses on the hyper-individualism that emerged on the social and political horizon at the end of the twentieth century.

A third hypothesis can be put forward in just a few words: the groundwork may also have been laid by the popularity of the *corporate identity* concept, which became extremely fashionable in the 1960s. Bring together expressions such as *corporate identity, corporate image,* and *brand image*, and it becomes logical and almost natural to end up with *brand identity*. Although the experts may have warned us against confusing the meaning of these expressions, their propinquity made exchanges and transferences among them inevitable.

A fourth possibility: brand identity having appeared about when mass marketing was reaching its peak, in the 1980s, as manufacturers and marketers were running out of creative ideas and being accused of having lost their soul, brand identity picked up where "soul" left off. Indeed, when they're not talking about DNA, many managers replace brand identity with words like "soul," "heart," and "essence."[23]

Still other hypotheses could be ventured, but this book isn't a work of scholarly research. Its goal is to try to understand how the concept of brand identity was formed—and then almost immediately deformed.

For the first thing that can be said about the subject is that everything happened very fast. Brand identity seemed to take over practically overnight, without any debates or hesitations, as something self-evident. And if it has parents, a birth date, and a birthplace, they're discreet to the point of invisibility.

WARNING: DEAD ENDS

The three impasses in which brand identity most often ends up can be presented more or less in the chronological order of their emergence. Let us note right off the bat that neither is a dead end in and of itself, but only to the extent that it presumes to embody the whole question of identity.

1. Brand identity is not just about a name, a product, or a logo

The practical-minded among my readers will tell me to stop splitting hairs. Things aren't so complicated. Someone's identity is what that someone is. That means brand identity is what the brand is, in other words what it makes, what it sells. Chrysler is a car brand, Dell a computer brand, Kellogg's a cereal brand, Levi's a jeans brand—and everything else is just idle chatter.

Except that what one does or makes is not enough to define what one is. Taken alone, the product doesn't define the brand, because it doesn't make it possible to distinguish that brand from the rest. By definition, a brand is distinct, unique. Drop two handfuls of cereal in a bowl of milk: who's to say they're Kellogg's? Look at the young man waiting for the bus on the sidewalk across the street: can you be absolutely sure that the jeans he's wearing are Levi's? Certainly not. Without the name on the product, in many cases it's difficult to identify the brand.

Fine, the same practical-minded folk will say, brand identity is made up of a product *and* a name. Yes, but that's not enough either. Max Factor possesses a famous name that is associated with a well-known line of products: it's a cosmetics brand. But that is not enough of an identity for it to fight against the competition, or at least that is the line of thinking that led Procter & Gamble to take the brand off American shelves in 2010.

Well, let's add the logo then. Lacoste is a sportswear brand that can be recognized by its little green crocodile. Shell is a gasoline brand that can be recognized by its red and yellow shell. Audi is a car brand that can be recognized by its four interlocking rings.

We're making progress, it's true, but neither Audi nor Shell nor Lacoste would be satisfied with such a definition of their identity. Audi, for example, is presented as follows by Interbrand:

> Audi is a brand that has no doubt about its identity, and that has transformed nonconformity into a virtue. The cars manufactured by the German maker

unabashedly display their own conception of prestige. Their target is also very clearly defined: an individualist who demands exceptional performance, who appreciates refinement rather than ostentation, who knows that technical excellence makes all the difference.[24]

The rest of the notice recalls Audi's history and that of its founder, the brand's place relative to the competition, and an overview of its advertising history. The word "cars" only appears once. What defines brand identity here is not a product but rather values, stances, attitudes: in other words, intangibles. Is this a more reliable approach? Not necessarily, as can be seen in the following exercise. Here are two other short excerpts from the same book:

X is unanimously recognized for its innovative design and for its cutting-edge products, which are at once aesthetically appealing and reliable.

Y is a world leader in its field, with a strong business culture centered on innovation and technical excellence.[25]

Were you able to guess the identity of these brands? Of course not, because neither Miele (the first) nor 3M (the second) has exclusive ownership of the values with which they are credited here.

It's not simplicity but simplemindedness to believe that material reference points (product, name, logo, and packaging) are sufficient to define the identity of a brand. And it is equally simpleminded, although seemingly more sophisticated, to think that nonmaterial reference points (values, visions, and commitments) define it any better.

Identity is always a combination of the two.

And it's the combination that's unique, not the individual elements. How many brands use a star, a globe, or a crown as an emblem? Probably dozens. But although the five-pointed Hallmark crown closely resembles the Rolex crown, there is never any confusion between them. How many brands use the same typographical characters? Also dozens. And the same colors? Shell, MasterCard, and Kodak are all yellow and red; Colgate, Levi's, and Canon are red and white; Chevron, Total, and Mobile are blue and red, just like the majority of the competition,[26] and hundreds of others are simply black and white, even within the same sector of the market.

However you look at the problem, what goes for brands also goes for cultures, countries, languages, and people: they are systems within which a few identical elements can give rise to an infinite number of possible combinations. Identity is the name that we give to such and such a specific combination, which is distinct from the others, and which we recognize whenever we encounter it.

2. Brand identity cannot be reduced to visual identity

This is the first, the oldest, and the most frequent of the dead ends. For many professionals, the only identity is a visual or "graphic" one. If you look for the word "identity" in the index of a book on brands, you'll almost always come up with "visual identity," generally defined with a formula something like this one:

> Visual identity: the sum of graphic elements—brand name, logo, emblem, label . . . that makes it possible to identify, to recognize at once a company, an organization, or a brand. These elements are described in detail in the house style guide.

Visual identity takes on even greater importance because it changes more often than before, and more radically. Instead of a logo and packaging that remain stable over time, scarcely touched up here and there (think of Chanel No. 5), today we are witnessing an acceleration in changes that are not only imposed by name changes resulting from mergers and acquisitions, but by the need to remain in step with a business environment that has been possessed, so to speak, by the demon of metamorphosis.

Obviously, nobody will dispute that what is called visual identity is a bearer of brand identity. When BP announced that it was changing its visual identity in September 2000, the operation went far beyond giving up its old insignia for a new logo. First of all, it was a matter of confirming the growth of the company after its merger with Amoco, Arco, and Castrol. Then, it was necessary to signify the growth of its centers of interest, and to break with the strictly oil-producing image of a group now turning more globally toward energy—whence the invitation to read its name as Beyond Petroleum. Finally, BP expressed a new desire—an ultra-delicate one in its sector of activity—to protect the environment and to adopt a more socially responsible attitude in producing countries. The result? A stylized flower (or a sort of sun, since the flower's nickname is Helios), colored white, yellow, and green, followed by the brand's two initials, no longer written in uppercase but in lowercase. Criticisms rained down from all sides when BP unveiled this pastoral image full of new intentions and too politically correct to be honest, coming from an oil-producing—ahem, energy—group. But at least its intentions were clear, and BP (bp) could justifiably speak of either identity or visual identity, without differentiating between the two: the one expressed the other, at least potentially.

But to treat the subject of identity exclusively from the angle of graphic choices (colors, forms, emblems, etc.) is singularly reductive, and sometimes even deceptive.

We must be very clear on this point: brand identity is *also* found in visual identity, but visual identity does not on its own embody brand identity. A logo is not a magic wand. It can do nothing against the sensations we feel while strolling through the aisles of a store, touching a fabric, turning over a label, standing in line at the cash register, nothing against (or for) the cleanliness of the carpet, the light, the music or the noise, the presence or absence of salespeople, their way of talking, responding, smiling—or ignoring their clients.

The visual identity of Air France is one thing, Air France's brand identity is another. To a certain extent it includes the well-known logo with its slanted blue, white, and red stripes, but it is also made up of all the interactions we may have with Air France, and in all probability these interactions play an even greater role in creating identity to the extent that they are personally experienced by the passengers. If one of them takes Air France for three straight flights, and each time the flight is late, in his or her eyes Air France's identity will be that of an airline whose flights are "always" late. The same goes for the visual identity of McDonald's: the big yellow M on a red background certainly had a big impact and did a good job helping customers find the restaurant, but in and of itself it expressed nothing in particular.[27] It is from repeated interaction with the brand that we take away a certain number of impressions, and not from the fact that its logo uses two warm colors (Kodak used the same two for a long time) or rounded lettering (many other brands do too).

On the other hand, if I have spent the winter in a pair of Geox that never let water in, that didn't change shape and took me to work as well as on my weekend trips without ever hurting my feet, all of this at a reasonable price while still being fashionable, Geox, for me, will stand for comfort, solid construction, and fashion, even if I don't know how to describe the brand's logo and have only the vaguest memory of the store where I purchased the boots and of the salesperson who assisted me.

Brand identity is a whole, its logic is hologramic, fractal.

Or as they say at Procter & Gamble: the devil is in the details. And British Airways wouldn't disagree. Its former president declared:

> Each time I take a flight, in other words at least once a week, I look around, I observe everything. For example, I pay attention to the announcements. If it's a flight to Frankfurt, does the flight crew speak in German, or are the announcements recorded? I look at the quality of the service, and not just of the meals.

I look at the inside of the plane, check to see if there are any broken seats, if there are stains on the carpet, and I do it without even thinking, because all of that is part of the brand.[28]

Visual identity is part and parcel of brand identity, but it is only one part. Price, products, advertising, the sales system, and each of the individuals who belongs to it in one way or another in the consumer's eyes all take part in forging that identity.

3. Brand identity has nothing to do with a genetic code

Having recently appeared in the remarks of numerous professionals, the genetic metaphor, one senses, tells marketing exactly what it wants to hear. It bespeaks a return to hard science in its most implacable incarnation: experiments, tests, calculations, figures, mathematical models, and, in the end, almost absolute certainty about the result.[29]

So we shouldn't be surprised to find constant references to the genetic code whenever a manager or a brand analyst addresses the question of identity:

The identity is a brand's DNA configuration, a particular set of brand elements, blended in a unique way, which determines how the brand will be perceived in the marketplace.[30]

Identity is the DNA structure of the brand.[31]

Upon the relaunching of Burberry, its new artistic director began by creating a little collection representing what he called "the prototype, the DNA" of the brand, and of its future. "We have to make fundamental changes to our approach," declared J. Nasser, president of Ford, before imposing on the old lady from Michigan a mutation that went far beyond a mere facelift: "We have to change our DNA!" "The company cannot delegate image creation to a third party," it was said at Benetton. "Otherwise, it would have to absorb the brand's DNA, which would take a lot of time and would be much more difficult for it than for us."

We know that an individual's genetic code is a "signature" that is so reliable that its analysis is now a part of all investigations where an individual's exact identity has to be determined.

But it's easy to make a logical leap and to conclude that an individual's identity boils down to his or her genetic code. We must obviously refrain from taking that leap: we know that genes are just a given, and that their carrier, by interacting with his or her environment, will develop a personality and a personal history that are impossible to predict in advance. We even know that the genome, contrary to popular opinion, can evolve over the course of an individual's life due to transcription errors. We cannot deduce what a person is like, nor what their future holds, from the mere fact that their genetic code makes it possible to identity them. In addition to the manipulations that it makes possible, DNA may perhaps be used as an "auxiliary of identity" in the sense the French civil code gives the phrase, but not in the sense in which it expresses an individual's unique personality.

It would be useless, in any case, to dwell on the success of the genetic metaphor: everyone has the sense that it's hard to extend very far, because when it comes right down to it, just what are the ingredients of this "brand DNA" that are supposed to contain the secret of its identity?

This question is usually answered by referring to "values" or certain qualities (pleasure, elegance, friendliness, confidence, and so on). None of these things is the exact equivalent of DNA, which, invisible to the naked eye though it may be, nonetheless possesses a very concrete and material existence. It is made up of nothing so intangible as a value or a quality: it is found on chromosomes. Now, what is the equivalent of a chromosome for Burberry, IBM, Colgate, or Gap?

The question is manifestly absurd.

What the comparison reveals, once more, is marketing's pronounced inclination for everything that approximates scientific law, for everything that seems capable of offering some semblance of certainty, for everything that can be controlled and manipulated, and for everything that looks like determinism.

A rational inclination, perhaps, but not a very reasonable one.

KEY POINTS

- Just as a goldfish is a fish before it is gold, brand identity belongs under the identity heading first and only second to the brand management category.

- Identity, such as it is studied today by the social sciences, appears as an unstable and fuzzy concept, whose popularity shouldn't make us forget how volatile it is.

- It follows that the identity concept should only be applied to brands with caution, taking into account the most recent work on the subject, and notably the research into identity's fluctuating character.

- We can now revise three of marketing's received ideas:

  ○ Brand identity is not the same thing as the name, the logo, or the products sold by the brand.

  ○ Brand identity cannot be reduced to visual identity.

  ○ It cannot be likened to some kind of brand "DNA," a pseudo-scientific analogy of little use for brand management.

CHAPTER 2

What's the State of Affairs Today?

Brand identity has a father—marketing—and a mother—the history of ideas. Knowing about both makes it possible to understand how this "concept" was born, how it developed, and the contradictions in which it remains tangled today. Once we understand its origins, it becomes easier to find a way of untangling those contradictions.

The concept of identity (before it was ever applied to brands) is a recent one, having emerged in the West only in the second half of the twentieth century.[1] Until then, the word just referred to the identical character of two objects, two people, or two groups. The specialists all agree that it was after World War II that it began to designate that which is both identical and stable in a human being or a social group throughout their existence, as well as what makes them unique and different from others. Infused with this paradoxical and psychological value, the word gradually infiltrated the media, politics, and then public opinion, where it passed for a concept that it probably isn't, for the reasons analyzed above.

It is thus far from being a universal concept. To the contrary, there is every reason to believe that some cultures have dispensed with it, and have been no worse off as a result. It is thus very possible that we are giving central importance to an idea that is destined to fade away in the coming decades, and that all of the surrounding ideas and corollaries will disappear with it, beginning with brand identity.

Until that happens, prudence demands all the same that we carefully examine this newcomer in the arena of marketing methods, if only to take as much advantage of it as possible without falling into any of the intellectual snares it has set for us.

FIGURE 1 | The Evolution of Marketing

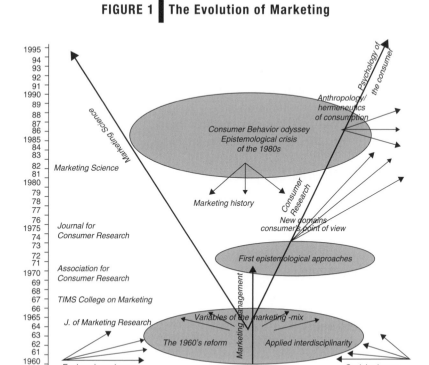

BRAND IDENTITY: A CONCEPT STRETCHED BETWEEN THE TWO BRANCHES OF MARKETING

This isn't a very comfortable position to be in, especially when the two branches in question aren't the same size and don't have the same strength. And yet this is what is happening, when one observes how brand identity is positioned on the tree of marketing as conceived since the 1960s.[2] (See Figure 1.)

It is apparent that after having grown more or less straight up for several decades, the trunk split around 1965 and divided into two: On the one hand, a single branch called marketing science; and on the other, another branch that is itself subdivided into a series of smaller branches: consumer research.

It's as if the first branch was inclining toward a return to the "engineering sciences" (bottom left of the diagram), while the second leaned toward the "social sciences" (bottom right). The American approach to marketing, which is the most well-known and the most used, can be located on the first branch, whereas in Europe, above all in Britain and France, marketers are following trails blazed by the humanities, which offer more opportunities for creativity.

The same bifurcation can be found in almost identical form in the difference between two conceptions of brand identity, one American, the other European, the first much better known, which justifies our examining it more closely.

Of the numerous publications on the subject, I'd like to focus on two, one explicit,[3] the other less so,[4] but both devoted to the question of brand identity.

The first book lists the components of identity as follows:

- product/service performance;

- name awareness;

- logo/graphic system;

- positioning;

- strategic personality;

- marketing communications;

- brand loyalty.

The second, which was published the following year, lengthens the list considerably, for it declares that brand identity is made up of twelve dimensions organized around four perspectives: the brand as a product, as an organization, as a person, and as a symbol. And, from the book's first page it is specified that brand *image* corresponds to how a brand is perceived, while brand *identity* is aspirational and represents how the brand would like to be perceived.

In other words, the brand is presented in two stages and in two forms: first we have what it "really" is—it's true identity, for which the company that manages it is responsible; and then we have its image, which is subjected to various distortions by consumers.

Numerous authors take up this definition more or less as is, stating that identity corresponds to the way a company wishes to present itself on the market, while image has to do with the public's associations.[5] For these authors, image is what the public receives, while identity is the message the brand sends out.[6]

A link is thus made between brand identity and the principles of "communication" as they are usually treated by marketing, that is to say superimposed on information theory and confused with it, since they share the same vocabulary:

- at the starting point, a "sender";

- in the middle, a message; and

- at the arrival point, a "receiver."

This is a mechanistic model, which is sometimes even called "telegraphic." It was developed by C. E. Shannon and W. Weaver at the end of the 1940s at Bell Laboratories and consisted in quantifying information with the help of bits, "by using already-existing mathematical tools from disciplines like thermodynamics and statistical mechanics." Strictly speaking, it has more to do with information technologies than with human communication, which adds a fundamental mechanism: feedback, as Norbert Wiener's research has shown.[7]

On the other hand, less known, mainly European, alternative models of brand identity, to which belongs the Fingerprint Method that will be explained later, tend to borrow from sociology, collective or individual psychology, linguistics (especially for brand core analysis and semiotic mapping), cognitive science, and, more recently, from evolutionary theory.

We thus have two different approaches to brand identity, located on two different branches of marketing, the one leaning toward the so-called exact sciences, the other toward the "social sciences" or "humanities." All of this seems extremely logical.

And yet something is missing. It's not something that jumps out at you at first glance, but in the midst of all this sound and fury swirling around the word "communication," where is communication theory, which forms the basis for the Fingerprint Method?

It's nowhere to be found, because dividing the branches in two has nothing to do with the communication theory vision of things. The researchers who laid the groundwork for communication theory came from a variety of disciplines in the sciences and the humanities and it was through dialogue among these disciplines that they moved forward, and not by defending the borders that separated them. To isolate the "social" and the "exact" sciences from each other was in their eyes utter nonsense. Breaking with the academic separation of knowledge, they sought to understand the mechanisms of communication by gathering and combining insights that came from anthropology, linguistics, psychology, and neurology. They all made abundant use of systems theory and the teachings of cybernetics.

Communication theory focused on the interaction between two interlocutors: and it is for this reason (among others) that it can help shed light on brands, which are a particularly complex example of interaction between companies and consumers. In essence, communication theory is a theory of links and relationships: dissociating or fragmenting knowledge is contrary to the communication theory approach.

If one adopts, as I have, the research and insights of this approach, it becomes impossible to choose one of the two brand identity visions, the one located on the marketing science branch, and the other on the consumer research branch. Nor can one reconcile them. Instead, one goes beyond them with the help of another kind of logic, non-separatist and more global: a logic that privileges a *systemic* conception of brands.

Consequently, the problem of brand identity can neither be properly posed nor resolved within the categories of classical marketing, even qualitative classical marketing.

In order to change the way we think, we have to change the words we use.

THE UNCONSCIOUS GETS INVOLVED

When Captain Cook arrived within sight of Oahu in January 1778, nobody in Hawaii could remember ever having seen vessels of that size and shape. The fishermen saw a strange silhouette with lights gliding across the ocean. They told the chief what they had seen, and the following day they saw it again, except closer this time. The huge sail both frightened and amazed the people, as did the giant masts and the sheer size of the vessel. There was much discussion, and various hypotheses were put forward about what this prodigious thing could be. Finally a priest silenced everyone by saying that it must be "the temple of Lono."[8]

Lono was one of the four main gods in the Hawaiian pantheon, and the priest's explanation was soon considered to be the only possible one, and it was made even more convincing by the fact that Cook's two boats had arrived via Kaelakekua Bay (in other words, by "the path of God"), and on the very day of the annual Festival of Lono. Cook received an absolutely sumptuous welcome: the Hawaiians had mistaken him for a God.

When we encounter something new, we react in the same way.[9] If memory doesn't shed light on an issue, we turn to imaginary, symbolic resources. We pull the unknown toward the known, we translate it into our language, ready to reduce, twist, and distort it until it fits into our categories of thought. Only then are we reassured—and then our problems begin, as they began for Hawaii when the English sailors started trading salt for fresh water, onions for poultry, various trinkets in exchange for various sums, and syphilis in exchange for a few caresses. Germs and illness went on to wreak terrible destruction: less than a century later, only a quarter of the original population remained. Today, 1 percent.

As for Cook, his promotion to the rank of living god lasted less than two weeks. No sooner had his two ships set out to sea again than a violent storm forced them to turn around. There was nobody left to welcome them on shore: the place where the festivities had taken place was now deemed taboo. The few Hawaiians they met didn't make the connection between these broken, exhausted men and Lono and his glorious crew. Their boats, open shells with broken masts and shredded sails, no longer looked much at all like floating temples. Were they usurpers? This time, relations began very inauspiciously, until a skirmish broke out during which Cook and several of his men were killed, then scalped, and horribly mutilated.

The moral of this tale? There are several, beginning with one more proof of our inexhaustible capacity, as human beings, for burning what we once worshipped. But here is one that we'll keep coming back to throughout this book: an object, an event (or a brand) have no meaning in and of themselves; they only acquire one through the play of circumstances, in other words in contexts.

How were brands understood and treated at first?

In the same way as the Hawaiians understood and treated the sudden appearance of Cook's ship: with the mental baggage at hand.

What was this baggage made up of? Of the dominant ideas, experiences, and prejudices of the era in which brands began to develop on a massive scale: in the United States, starting in the last third of the nineteenth century and continuing into the middle of the twentieth.

Of course, Europe had also seen the birth of numerous brands during the same period (for example Shell and Michelin in 1890, Nestlé in 1866, Fiat in 1899) and even much earlier: Maille was born in 1747, Guinness in 1789, and Twining's in 1706. But the phenomenon never attained the proportions that it immediately assumed in the United States. Similarly, even though the first industrial revolution took place in England in the eighteenth century, it was in the United States a century later that it reached the height of its strength, and in Germany and Great Britain as well. And it's there that the mental baggage referred to above can be found.

A single word sums it up nicely, and more precisely a verb, and an action verb at that: to build.

What was built? Edifices, at first. Farms, barns, and then houses, stores, warehouses, and soon factories, apartment buildings, neighborhoods, harbors, entire cities. Then roads and railways. The idea was to divide up the immense territory into an increasingly tightly-knit transportation network.

And finally, factories. And these factories in turn built boats and steam engines, and then automobiles, but also stoves, iceboxes, carts, and machines. Thousands of machines—sewing machines, typewriters, calculators, weaving machines, soldering irons, hole-punchers—machines to do everything faster, better, and for less than by hand.

IN THE BEGINNING WERE THE ROCK BRAND AND THE MACHINE BRAND

In this context, there's nothing surprising about the fact that the symbolism and imagery surrounding brands started by borrowing from architecture and industry, together or separately: this is what I described[10] by sketching a lineage that went from the rock brand to the edifice brand and then to the motor or machine brand. All the examples that I cited then are still valid today, and many others have since appeared, confirming contemporary marketing's predilection (and that of the business world in general) for a vision of brands steeped in architectural symbolism and imagery. Shall we give a few samples?

"The three pillars of the brand: innovation, fun, and personal satisfaction," says Reebok. At Uncle Ben's, the "two pillars of the brand are innovation and practicality". Longines has three: traditional clock-making, chronometers for sports, and industrial electronics.

This confirms that architectural metaphors and symbols continue, even today, to dominate our conception of brands, even though the Second Wave,[11] to which these metaphors and symbols belonged, has vanished, and the Third, the information era, makes it possible to imagine a Fourth that will be just as powerful as its predecessors, if not more so.[12]

Procter & Gamble spares no effort to adapt to the new millennium, but when, in 1998, one of its managers published a book that promised to reveal the 99 principles on which the success of P&G depends,[13] he insisted on the fact that most of those principles, could be traced back to the company's founders, W. Procter and J. Gamble.[14] Allow me to cite three of the book's chapters: "Build Superior Products," "Build Enduring Company Relationships," and "Build Long-Term Profit." Let us recall the titles of two other books that I have been citing frequently: *Building Strong Brands* and *Building Brand Identity*, not to mention *Built to Last*.[15] And let's not forget the popular expression "brand architecture," which pops up on every other page of these various books as well as in the literature on brands in general (including the books produced by advertising agencies for their internal use).

As for brands, even the most recent and those that are looking to change the most, continue to draw on the same sources: Renault, which one might have thought would be naturally drawn to a machine-inspired image, depicts its brand identity in the form of a pyramid—an image of which P. Brabeck, at Nestlé, was equally fond.

And yet, an edifice is immobile. A motor or a machine doesn't work unless a person operates it: once he or she stops, the machine stops too. Whereas brands, oddly, keep moving forward even when nobody is at the helm, as if they were endowed with a life of their own. It's a well-known phenomenon and measured by all of the best-known studies: even brands that have been abandoned or put to rest for ten, fifteen, twenty, or even more years continue to live in the memories of consumers, in the absence of all advertising, all presence on the shelf, all trace of current activity. In this way, unexpected resurrections sometimes happen, as if brands had acquired a capacity that machines lack: that of being endowed with a mysterious form of life. The automaton ends up starting to walk, to move, to speak—to live a life of its own. What can we conclude from this? That brands can also borrow from another symbolic and imaginary source: the human person.

THEN CAME THE STAR BRAND AND THE PERSON BRAND

Between the Machine Brand and the Person Brand, in France, there was the Star Brand, theorized in the form of Star-Strategy

A complete description of the Star Strategy, which was very influential at the time, can be found in *Hollywood lave plus blanc*,[16] published in 1982 and written by French advertising guru Jacques Séguéla. The idea is based on a simple principle: "Brands are like stars" but not just any kind of movie star: stars from the heyday of Hollywood, the glorious period that stretched from the 1930s to the 1960s or 1970s. Star-strategy is thus clearly a part of what Guy Debord called the society of the spectacle, except that Debord's book was "consciously written with the intention of causing harm to spectacular society,"[17] while Star-strategy aimed to accelerate its advent, illustrating Chapter 2 of Debord's book after the fact: merchandise as spectacle.

The idea that a brand cannot be inert like a machine but endowed with a personality, like an individual, was the point of departure for Star-Strategy, and this was seen by the inventor as a deliberate reaction against the mechanistic, American approach. We might even speak of a revolt against the narrow framework that prevailed at the time in the advertising agencies, a framework imposed by the so-called USP (Unique Selling Proposition) model. In Jacques Séguéla's opinion, this model had three weaknesses, one of which, the last, was fatal: it was repressive, it was exclusively rational, and it was materialist. It had to be changed. The decision was thus made:

> ...to refuse ever to speak of brands. We would speak instead of person brands.[18]

And this was more than just a reflexive spasm of ill-humor against American hegemony:

> The idea is not as new as its systematization. Already, B. Bernbach, furious with the white-collar workers of Procter & Gamble, the biggest detergent producer in the world, had cried out his disagreement at the beginning of the 1970s: "The technocrats of Madison Avenue can create a body, but they're incapable of making blood run in its veins."[19]

And so the brand became a star, helping lots of French and European companies develop increasingly spectacular media strategies, in accord with the spirit of the 1980s and its taste for over-the-top advertising, which was often very glamorous and marked a decisive turn toward celebrity marketing.

The problem was that, while he thought he was correcting American marketing's overly mechanistic tendencies by adopting a more "human" model, Séguéla fell into the exact same trap.

Stars, as we've known for a long time, are industrial products just like any other, fabricated by show-business using the same methods and with the same goals as with detergents in the detergent industry, cars in the car industry, and cereals in the food industry. They thus have no trouble being integrated into the spectacle of advertising, acting just like machine brands, born of a mechanistic and industrial logic, even though they look like person brands.[20]

Star status is only obtained at the cost of forgetting that behind the star there is a person (as stars themselves take it upon themselves to remind us when they are interviewed). And thus the person brand, having stepped down from the star pedestal, made it possible for marketing to move a little closer to a conception of identity borrowed directly from human identity.

But what human identity? What person? What vision of mankind lies behind contemporary marketing literature?

Behind the rock brand and the edifice brand there is the civilizing ideology and the desire for immortality. Behind the brand-machine and the
brand-motor, there is the productivist ideology and the mythology of
progress. What lies behind the person brand?

That's harder to discern for two reasons:

■ We're closer to it and thus lack critical distance for analyzing it;

■ Without the attributes and glitter of the star, the person brand amounts to
  nothing concrete. The brand-machine and the brand-edifice are objects,
  and objects stimulate the imagination. The person brand is very hard to
  visualize.

Why? Because the "person" is just that: any old individual, and thus banal,
or else (at least in French) an absence. Moreover, this "person" that gives
brands its symbolic imagery and its model of functioning is paradoxically
rather hollow:

> Each generation likes to recognize itself and to find its identity in a great mytho-
> logical or legendary figure that it reinterprets according to the problems it faces:
> Oedipus as a universal emblem, Prometheus, Faust and Sisyphus as mirrors of the
> human condition. Today, it's Narcissus who, in the eyes of a great many researchers,
> especially American ones, symbolizes the present.[21]

Narcissus, as we know, by dint of admiring his image reflected in the river,
fell in and drowned. The myth's "lesson" is fairly clear: when the hyper-
individualist looks to the horizon, all he sees is himself, and this tête-à-tête
with oneself inevitably proves fatal. There may be external solutions against
this danger, against this void, such as plunging collectively into the great
tribal "magma," as described in *The Time of the Tribe*.[22]

But there may also be solutions that come "from within" in a certain
sense. We are persuaded— although it's a rather recent conviction—that we
are structured internally by something like a framework, a sort of psychological skeleton that makes us into a unique and autonomous human being,
and that we call identity. We are also persuaded that it is our responsibility
to explore, protect, and make others respect this identity—by force, if necessary. We have the right to know who we are and the right to defend that
identity. Nothing that we do in its name can earn us the slightest reproach:
such is the contemporary orthodoxy.

There isn't a single magazine, TV series, or talk show that doesn't do
its best to drive this idea into our heads: know who you are, be yourself,

assert yourself, defend your identity, in the name of which you are entitled to just about every right. A brand like Calvin Klein drew the logical conclusion from this trend and launched the perfume CK Be, which seeks to embody this trend toward assertiveness. Hugo Boss says the same thing in other terms: "Don't imitate, innovate." Lacoste went even further, borrowing Nietzsche's famous "Become who you are." And in the business world, all the techniques for personal development are based on the idea that being assertive is the first step toward a positive change in professional behavior.

The consequence: if brands are seen as persons, and if the vocation of the person is to assert him or herself, then brands are also called to become intimately acquainted with and to accept their identity, and if need be, to assert it.

We were wondering what ideology was hiding behind the person brand, and now it's becoming apparent. For beyond the Socratic "Know thyself," the question is: for what purpose? Not for pure curiosity's sake, but rather so as to have a reason for asserting oneself, for defending one's positions, for occupying the space to which one is entitled. In short, so as to exist and to compel others (consumers, in this instance) to recognize that existence, such that they "identify" the brand in turn—in other words, so that they make a clear distinction between your brand and the competition.

Identity is a weapon, for individuals as for nations. A defensive weapon, a shield behind which one takes refuge to justify what one does, or else an offensive weapon, as when one launches a rebellion or a war in the name of such and such an identity.[23] In its name, every battle is legitimized, every fight is a glorious one. The advantage of the identity concept is its almost spontaneously adversarial character.

And the same goes for brand identity. The "marketing warfare"[24] that companies prize so highly is only meaningful to the extent that brands are adversaries, whence the thesis (or even the apology) of their indispensable differentiation. And what better instrument of differentiation than identity? In its name, attacks are carried out, threats made, assaults undertaken, and even murders committed, as numerous conflicts around the globe demonstrate, even in Europe.[25] If this is how things play out among humans, and if brands are persons, it follows that, in imitation of its model, brands are entitled to fight—and to combat others—in the name of their identity.

The person brand as it is conceived today clearly goes along with the liberal economy and its competitive clashes. It would therefore be wrong to fall into the trap of thinking that brands are somehow being "humanized" simply because they are comparing themselves to "persons." It would be equally wrong to think that for this reason person brands are better suited to the logic of communication than the brand-edifice or the brand-machine.

Is proof necessary? All one has to do is look at the way the person brand is depicted in the various publications that describe it.

USING GEOMETRY TO DEFINE IDENTITY

No "object" such as a motor or a machine is used to depict or symbolize brand identity yet identity is not an entirely abstract concept. A closer look reveals that two geometrical figures are in favor with the theoreticians, and these two figures reveal a great deal about the way marketing conceives of identity in general, and brand identity in particular.

In terms of symbolic charge, a geometrical figure can say just as much as an animal or an object, even if it seems a little dry and abstract at first glance. A cypress, a bear, or a star can "speak" directly or indirectly to the imagination. A straight line, a rhombus, or an ellipse are not quite so immediately evocative.

And yet the four primary geometrical figures, the ones from which almost all the others are derived (the square, the circle, the center, and the cross) have a very powerful symbolic charge. In its simplest form, the cross, for example—which can also be combined with the other three—can be linked to earth symbolism and thus to the number 4. In designating the four cardinal points, it represents the principle of orientation, but also intersection, crossing, and meeting, which gives it something in common with the bridge symbol (bridge = that which links), as well as with the ladder or the tree (which rises into the sky, linking human beings to God).

Brand identity tends to adopt two of these fundamental geometrical figures. The first one is the circle, or, more precisely, the center and the circle, the first inside and in the middle of the second.[26] Now, we know that the circle, like the point (the one being an extension of the other) is a symbol for totality, perfection, and homogeneity: a bit of these three qualities can be perceived in the way brand identity is depicted in these various—and yet similar—figures. We know also that concentric circles stand for hierarchy, which means that brand identity, when it is depicted this way, is seen as graduated, with maximum levels of concentration at the system's center, and dilution as one heads outward. Brand identity thus appears to contain what is most important at its core.

The other geometrical figure that dominates depictions of brand identity is the triangle. It is harder to spot because:

- it appears less frequently than concentric circles;

- it often appears in the guise of a triangle that is partly hidden or distorted.

The classic triangle, for its part—that is to say the equilateral triangle, point upward—is more highly prized by marketing in general, which finds it particularly irresistible, either for depicting a hierarchy or for describing questions of identity. Marketing literature also provides many examples in which the equilateral triangle is used to illustrate brand identity.[27]

The triangle lends itself particularly well to the architectural imaginary: the angle bracket is at once a triangular instrument and a symbol, and the pyramid is the most striking incarnation of the shape, since each facet has a triangular form. The brand-edifice thus finds in the triangle the best possible representation of its identity, in the form of a graduated set of "Ideals" that progresses by degrees toward what is most essential. Several big brands have chosen to represent their identity in the form of a pyramid, sometimes even giving it a "base," for greater security. Their internal documents take it upon themselves to get this message across in big, beautiful color drawings, and the diagram's simplicity certainly makes it readily understandable and facilitates adoption by staff unfamiliar with the brand's logic.

The triangle is thus indeed the second major geometrical figure that dominates depictions of brand identity. It is no less symbolically rich than the circle, and its spiritual dimension is no less obvious. The principal difference between them is that the circle embodies a self-sufficient fullness, while the triangle can be understood in relation to other geometrical figures: it engenders the square, which itself engenders the pentagon, and so on, which makes it more dynamic than the circle, which has neither beginning nor end and more easily symbolizes time—but a ceaselessly repeated time, in other words, infinity.

We might conclude from this that circular representations tend toward invariability and suggest that brand identity is something intangible and absolute, while triangular representations entail a more concrete, lively, and evolution-oriented conception of brand identity.

But we're going to see that these distinctions disappear in the face of troubling similarities.

DO BRANDS POSSESS AN "ESSENCE"?

In principle, the triangle and the circle are two distinct figures: it follows that the two conceptions of brand identity that they illustrate should also be distinct.

Yet if we take a look at the most recent of these models, the so-called brand core analysis model, which I will be discussing later on, what do we see? That its upper portion is tinted, as if it were denser than the rest. Moreover, it is situated at the peak of the "triangle".

What is the name of this peak? The "symbolic core." And its form? A circle.

In other words, in the guise of two different geometrical forms, we're dealing with two conceptions of brand identity that are closer to each other than they first appeared.

In fact, whether one turns the spotlight on the center of a circle or the summit of a pyramid, assigning to center and summit a superior power of concentration, the same operation takes place: a distinction between what is essential and what is less so. It is, indeed, very difficult to mark a division between two or more components of identity without succumbing to the (conscious or unconscious) temptation to hierarchize them with respect to one another. To inscribe and color a little circle inside a bigger one amounts to drawing a focal point, implicitly ascribing more value to it than to the rest.

The commentators are clear on this point:

> The peak is the brand's core identity, the source of identity.[28]

> Brand identity structure includes a core and extended identity. The core identity—the central, timeless essence of the brand—is most likely to remain constant as the brand travels to new markets and products.[29]

Here we see a new lexical slippage that starts from the notion of "core" (which also means "heart" and "center") and moves toward the "profound nature" of the brand, often called its "essence". In *Prince of the Magic Kingdom,* J. Flower writes that for Disney, the core of the brand is formed by a cluster of images: Walt Disney, theme parks, Mickey, Minnie, and the idea of family fun.[30]

Between essence and soul there is but a small distance—a distance that marketing didn't take long to cover. In his book *Mythmaking on Madison Avenue*, S. Randazzo notes that a brand can even have a "soul," which he defines as "its spiritual center, the core values that define the brand and permeate all of its other features."[31] Clearly, identity, essence, and soul are three words for one idea, whether that idea is explained with the vocabulary of psychology and sociology (identity), philosophy (essence), or religion (soul). It is as if marketing, without giving up its mechanistic origins, since it continues to describe brands as "cash machines," was trying to inject something human into them, at the cost of some rather high-flying conceptual acrobatics. Or perhaps marketing is drawing here on symbolism inspired not by science but by science fiction, a domain where hybrids are everywhere and where men and machines exchange properties that are usually the privilege of either one or the other.

In any event, no matter what angle of attack is adopted, one arrives at the same observations:

- Brand identity is depicted with the aid of geometric figures: either the circle or the triangle. These geometric figures are closed and are organized around a center, which is denser than the rest.

- This center contains what is most precious about the brand's identity: its "essence."

- It follows that, just like "essence," brand identity is non-material, unalterable, and sacred.

- It also follows that the brand's "essence" has greater value than its existence (or its successive existences).

This conception of brand identity has been accepted all the more readily because it very closely resembles the idea that each of us has of identity in the larger sense, even if this idea is only an approximation. In short, it is consistent with all the received ideas—and to this it owes a good part of its success.

Received ideas are useful in their place. This one, however, is deceptive: first of all, there is not just one classical conception of identity in Western cultures, but two; and then, the reasons for which one of the two dominated the other for a long time are now in the process of changing.

A quick word on these two conceptions of identity. They were both born at about the same time, in the sixth and fifth centuries BC, and they have survived until now, in various forms and with varied success. To summarize them crudely, let us call the ghost of Jean-Paul Sartre to our rescue and employ his cherished vocabulary:

> [T]o my right, "essence," something innate and immutable in a human being that makes it possible for him or her to remain the same over time, and that thus grounds his or her identity; to my left, "existence," plunged in the shimmering changeability of daily life with its thousand and one reversals, which produce a myriad of different identities in the same individual.[32]

If marketing thought that existence preceded essence, it would be existentialist. But it thinks the contrary: it is therefore essentialist, which leads it to adopt a certain vision of brand identity. Whether it knows it or not, whether it accepts it or not, it really does have a philosophical position on the subject.

That position is the following: the brand is a person. What distinguishes a person, in other words a human being, from all other animals, even the "higher" apes, is the possession of consciousness, reason, and spirit, perhaps even a soul. Thus Seat, a Spanish car brand, has declares that is has "a Latin soul." By the same token, Guerlain has been presenting itself for a long time as being "the soul of perfume."

The advantage of possessing a soul is obvious: the soul is immortal. But the word has a connotation that is too mystical for a secular religion like marketing: it thus has to be translated in terms of identity. And, quite automatically, the same relationship is established between the identity and the brand as between the soul and the body, spirit and matter: the one can grow old, but not the other. The one can change, the other is eternal. The one is mortal, the other is not. This, at least, is the dominant line of thinking in the West since Plato.

It is this line of thinking that explains the systematic preference for pyramids divided into material layers (at the bottom) and spiritual ones (at the top), as is the case for Maslow's classic pyramid. In the same way, that which is most specific and precious to human beings—the spirit or the "soul"—will be depicted on the top and in the center of a diagram, which amounts to the same thing, since the center is often represented by an elevation, a mountain for example.

Marketing was born in America, a religious country without a clear and legal frontier between the State and the Church. And the first American advertising agencies recruited many managers who had a background in the priesthood, which is logical when one remembers that propaganda[33] is a technique with religious, and, more precisely, Christian origins. It is to this lineage that we can trace the source of an idealism that contrasts violently with the hyper-materialism that prevails in American business circles. Max Weber has explained why the two go hand in hand. Transferred to brands, this idealism explains why the question of identity is always brought back to essence rather than to existence, whence the irrepressible tendency to clothe it in an evanescent or even evangelical vocabulary, which in either case is unlikely to promote rationality.

KEY POINTS

■ In the course of their history, brands have been successively depicted as

   ○ Buildings (solidity)

   ○ Machines (productivity)

- ○ Movie stars (power of attraction)

- ○ Persons (autonomy)

- ■ Their identity often takes symbolic form:

  - ○ A circle (identity occupies the center);

  - ○ A triangle (identity occupies the center or the summit)

- ■ Brand identity is thus invested with meanings that go way beyond its use as a tool for strategic analysis, as attested by the philosophical and religious vocabulary that accompanies the concept (essence, heart, and soul).

- ■ This over-investment presents an obstacle both to critical thinking and to the necessity of rethinking brand identity: it is thus desirable to do away with it.

CHAPTER 3

Redefining Brand Identity

> We must deconstruct, of course, but on condition that we also reconstruct. There is no lack of research that can help us to forge a better understanding of the notion of identity. This research is equally fertile when it is transferred to the world of brands, where it makes possible a stimulating redefinition of brand identity.

"Everything excessive is insignificant," said Talleyrand, the fearsome and feared minister in Napoleon's government. The excesses of materialism are just as bad as those of spiritualism. The two can be observed in real time on every American television station, where the sermons, Christian or otherwise, on the need for moderation and spiritual elevation are intercut with incessant calls to go out and buy, buy, buy. Sometimes, when the preachers sell books, DVDs, and tickets to their shows, and brands sell love, happiness, and peace of mind, it's hard to know where the sermons end and the advertisements begin.

Brand identity is also victim of materialist excesses, as witnessed by marketing's obsession with DNA, but also spiritualist excesses, with marketing's lyrical flights about the "essence" or "soul" of the brand, whose fleeting existence is a poor cover for its underlying emptiness.

Is it possible to escape these two traps?

Yes, but to do so we must leave our mental comfort zone.

HOW I CHANGED MY MIND ABOUT BRAND IDENTITY

Experience and the practice of conducting studies on brand identity were what gradually led me to change my mind on the subject. In the space of fifteen years, I must have made at least fifty such studies, and I saw at least as many, if not more, being made by advertising agencies and consultancies, using different methods and with varied objectives.

In general, it's not very hard to convince people that such an exercise is useful, and as always, the best argument consists in citing an example. In France, there was one that was cited so often that it became practically canonical. I'll give a rapid summary of the story here, as it was generally told.

In the early 1980s, Fidji was one of the best-selling perfumes in the world. Its owner, L'Oréal, not wishing to rest on its laurels, began thinking about how to improve the perfume's advertising image. Until then, the image was a very chaste photograph of a nude woman, her eyes closed, kneeling on a beach where the water meets the sand, holding in her arms a large bottle of perfume. The slogan was just as well-known and well-liked as the photo: "Woman is an island. Fidji is her perfume."

The image was used with excellent results for several years, until the company began to fear that it was no longer in touch with its era. And it must be said that things were changing very quickly: increasingly daring female figures were popping up all around us (the sexual revolution was accomplishing its aims), along with increasingly exotic dreams about the ideal vacation locale (the leisure revolution was also beginning to gain ground). The success of Club Med bore witness to the strength of these two trends and made them even stronger.

It was thus decided to change Fidji's image, and to bring it up to speed with modernity. There appeared the frontal portrait of a sultry Tahitian endowed with some suggestive symbols: an abundant head of thick, curly black hair, bright red lips, an orchid (also red) tucked behind her ear, and a snake wrapped around her throat like a necklace. In her hands, standing straight up, she held a bottle of Fidji.

Sales plummeted.

What had happened? Answer: an utter misunderstanding. The provocative tropical Eve, whose presence seemed so natural for a perfume called Fidji, was an unwelcome intrusion in the imaginations of female consumers.

What had attracted them in the past was not the exoticism of the image (which was in any event not in the least exotic), but a distant world closed off to the outside, an unexplored continent, a virgin island, and moreover, a sort of mother figure. Anything, that is, but a sensual playgirl.

In other words, it was a case of mistaken identity. Fidji's identity was timeless and had nothing to do with modernity or exoticism. Wanting at all costs to shove it back into a given timeframe (the 1980s) and a given place (Polynesia) was to reduce it to something quite insignificant compared to the powerful symbolic condensation that it had achieved before. The plummeting sales were ample proof that one does not play fast and loose with brand identity. None of the attempts undertaken to return Fidji to its initial illustrious status, not even the reinforcement provided by a supermodel who was then at the height of her fame, could make the brand successful again.

I myself have often cited this example because its illustrative power appeared so striking. And then, little by little, I began to have nagging doubts, and this for two reasons:

■ When one went back to the original sources, that is to say to the case study of Fidji, one saw that things were not as clear as they seemed, and that the summaries made here and there simplified the story egregiously. The plummeting sales may have been due to other causes (such as problems of distribution or varying exchange rates in Asia) rather than to the change in identity;

■ This identity was presented as having been entirely constructed by advertising, although it is well known that advertising is never the only thing responsible for what happens in the life of a brand. Even if in some sectors, such as perfume, it is obvious that image plays an important role, this image is fashioned not only by the magic of advertising, but also upstream, downstream, and on all sides of advertising. Therefore, I couldn't keep basing my viewpoint on an example in which advertising was given more weight than the other components of the brand.

Each day, the emblematic example of Fidji lost a little more of its credibility in my eyes.

But that wasn't the only reason that led me to reflect more deeply about the question of brand identity.

During this period, over the course of various books, articles, and lectures, I witnessed the construction of a discourse on brand identity which seemed irreproachable to me at first. Yet here, too, I gradually became more skeptical. The more I observed the life of brands, the less that life seemed to correspond to the postulates of the collective mentality.

What were the ingredients of this discourse?

It revolved (and still revolves, last I heard) around a tiny number of leitmotifs that I listed above: brand identity is fixed in place and shouldn't change, it is intangible, fragile, the property of the company, and it can be understand in comparison with the human psyche, etc.

But even as these themes were being developed here and there, one would have had to be blind not to notice that:

■ Brand identity is not fixed in place. Lancia used to be a young, sporty brand; now it's a posh, indeed almost a bourgeois, brand. Hermès no longer has much in common with the doddering old leather goods dealer that it still was in the 1970s. Helena Rubinstein has been in succession an innovative American brand, an old-fashioned, lifeless brand, and an international, avant-garde brand—and so on and so forth. The list could go on for pages.

■ Brand identity is not as fragile as is commonly thought. Lanvin is still alive and well, despite a catastrophic series of changes in its stakeholders, directors, and strategies. And not only is brand identity not fragile, but in many cases it is on the contrary its strength that causes problems, to the extent that it constitutes an obstacle to change.

■ Brand identity is not intangible. Jaguar's identity doesn't float like a perfume in the wake of the brand. It is not made up exclusively of rarefied values like elegance and elitism. No, it is made up of steel, wood, leather, and of certain lines unique to the design of Jaguar. Danone's identity is linked to plain yogurt. Diesel's identity is not only made up of fashion and provocation, but also of ready-to-wear clothing. Brands have a body and this body forms a part of their identity, neither more nor less than the rest.

■ Brand identity does not belong to the company, because brands are jointly held properties that the consumers also manage, even if they do not realize this. Neither Lacoste nor Helly Hansen nor Timberland was able to do anything about the fact that young clients were putting their brand to a use that was more urban than intended, and because these clients were an integral part of the brand, the image and thus the identity of all three (company, brand, and clients) was necessarily altered.

■ A brand is not a person. No matter how you look at it, this is just a comparison, nothing more. It cannot be taken too far without the risk of coming up with absurdities that are at best amusing, at worse inept, and in any case not in the least applicable to reality.

Thus, from all sides, my first convictions about brand identity started to crumble under the pressure of the numerous counterexamples that I saw all around me on a daily basis. Nor was I the only one to criticize these received ideas, which for the most part were imported from the US. A handful of European specialists also began to oppose them, such as A. Semprini, who asserted that brand identity "does not belong exclusively to the company":

> For a long time we have had a tendency to attribute the right and power to found brand identity exclusively to the company. The reality of the marketplace shows

that after a certain period of time a brand often possesses an identity that is different from the one that the company decided to give it.[1]

But the biggest stumbling block came from the contradiction between what I saw around me and my own conception of brands, which was based on the systemic approach,[2] the first consequence of which for me was going beyond the "Sender → Message → Receiver" model.

This model is simple, clear, easy to use, and, above all, deeply anchored in the marketing culture. But one has to be logical: if one believes that brands are made up of communication, it is necessary to turn to communication theory, and not information technologies.

If we follow Karl Popper's reasoning, and look at brands as evolving systems,[3] it is easier to realize that there is nothing immutable, nothing static about them or their identity. To the extent that a cloud is an open, dynamic, and complex system, it may be composed of constants, but not of fixed points. A cloud doesn't have a stable identity. It can change shapes several times and still be the same cloud for the one who is observing its evolution over the course of several minutes.

Club Med has been in succession, and sometimes simultaneously, democratic and elitist, individualist and family-oriented, nomadic and sedentary, French and cosmopolitan, one of a kind and copied by everyone, foreign vacation spot and city leisure center. Does it remain Club Med? Yes. Does it always have the same identity? Not really.

What then was to be done with the notion of brand identity such as it is usually understood, which is to say as something centripetal, intangible, static, and untouchable?

Answer: this notion had to be radically changed, because it was obviously inadequate.

REVOLUTIONIZING OUR UNDERSTANDING OF BRAND IDENTITY

To what and to whom shall we turn in order to revolutionize our understanding of brand identity and detach it both from its spiritualist excesses and from the false science and fanaticism at work behind so-called Brand DNA? To the human and social sciences, if we think that only human beings have an identity.

What do recent studies about identity tell us? Several things, which strike a blow against most received ideas on the subject. For example:

- There is no identity "in and of itself"; identity doesn't exist by itself, it is not a fixed "something" at the heart of another "something" that is capable of change. To put it in philosophical terms, identity is not an immutable "essence" that transcends being and existence.

- It is a concept at the crossroads: no one science can presume to provide a definition unless it adopts a transdisciplinary approach.

- Identity is polymorphous. "We live in the illusion that identity is one and indivisible, when in reality it is always a *unitas multiplex*. We all have multiple identities."[4]

- Identity is "a process that unfolds throughout the life" of an individual. We should speak not of "content" but of an "identity dynamic"[5] that evolves and rearranges itself continually, passing through a series of crises and stages.

- An individual's identity comes from without, and not (or not only) from within. It depends on the context in which the individual lives and develops. It is not innate but acquired through interactions and relationships with others and with the environment. There is no identity without otherness.

If we take up each of these points and apply them to brand identity, what must we conclude?

- That marketing should change its way of conceiving brand identity (and as it deduces brand identity from what it knows about human identity, its vision of the latter should also change—but since nobody is required to do the impossible, it would be enough to change its vision of the former, which would be an accomplishment in itself).

- That brand identity isn't defined as a nonmaterial, impalpable "essence". It is located in the "body" as much as in the "mind" of the brand, without distinction or hierarchy between them.

- That the question of the "content" of brand identity is less relevant than the question of the relational system from which it emerged.

- That neither psychology, sociology, cognitive science, nor semiology holds the key to brand identity: each has part of the key, but none has it all. Only a transdisciplinary approach that integrates these various approaches (and others too) can have any chance of grasping such a complex notion.

- That (as a result) we have to acknowledge this complexity, stop trying to domesticate it with rationalist logic, and accept that we can't control it completely. Here the mythology of power and will that undergirds the whole marketing culture runs into a reality that's hard to decode, hard to control, and in any event resistant to simplistic reductions.

In IBM's identity there is as much blue as power and technology. In McDonald's identity, there is as much hamburger as happiness. In Chanel's identity there is a tweed suit, elegance, quilted handbags, the rejection of convention, N° 5, classicism as far as the clothing goes, baroque for the accessories, or sometimes the opposite, navy, beige, black and white, the memory of Coco, Karl Lagerfeld's insolence, a camellia, the Ritz, a boater, and so forth.

In short, a brand and its identity belong to the category of hybrids, a domain that contemporary science and technology are just beginning to explore, a domain that has already produced numerous discoveries, such as composite materials, and that is based on the following first principle of systems theory: bringing together two or more materials, which can be of natural or artificial origin and present in very unequal doses, produces new properties that were not observable in any of the individual materials. This is, once again, a verification of the principle that the whole is superior to, or at least different from, the sum of its parts, and that a system's behavior cannot be explained by adding up the different behaviors of its constitutive elements.

This is word for word what we could say about brands and their identity, as with everything that can be analyzed as a human, or at least a living, system.

Can we go beyond analysis and observe living mechanisms not just in order to recognize and understand them but also to repair them, for example, or to imitate them, at least to learn lessons that are applicable to many areas, including the very concrete and pragmatic world of marketing and its tools?

WHAT IF THERE WERE SEVERAL CORES?

As we have seen, almost all conceptions of brand identity converge toward a "core identity" while basing their conclusions on cognitive science.

Brands could learn a lot from cognitive science, which studies, for example, how perception, memory, attention, and language function. Cognitive science is hard to get a grasp on, and hard to understand, but we should at least keep in mind that from the beginning it broke with the habit of ascribing solely to psychology the task of understanding how the human mind functions. If there existed such a thing as a "physics of thought," cognitive science would be it. It was born in the 1940s, at the same time as cybernetics, at the impetus of the same researchers (N. Wiener, J. von Neumann, A. M. Turing, and McCulloch) with the help of mathematical logic, with, as a first achievement, the birth of the computer and research on artificial intelligence.

Naturally, marketing is very interested in cognitive science, even having gone so far as to invent "neuromarketing." We do not as yet know what this new discipline may become. We know only that it has scientific pretensions, and that these pretensions offer professionals the comfort of being able to reason once more (rightly or wrongly) in mechanistic terms, that is to say by looking at the brain as a machine whose workings will soon be completely understood. Emotions, memory, and perceptions will then be controllable at will—such, at least, is the unacknowledged dream of neuro-marketing. Many companies are apparently already interested, but—apart from DaimlerChrysler—without saying so, for fear of a backlash. Indeed, several consumer advocacy sites are already on alert, ready to defuse one by one every attempt to use new technologies for brain exploration to hack into the inner recesses of our minds. For the moment, they don't have a whole lot of work.

Better, then, to concentrate on what cognitive science can provide us without posing any threat to our free will.

We know that cognitive science often uses the notion of "representation." But we have to be careful: despite its humble appearance, the word takes on a very technical sense here. Computers manipulate "symbols ([…] elements that represent what they stand for). The key notion here is that of representation…"[6] How is the mental representation of a tree formed? Or the representation of the notion of city? How is the category "taxi driver" constructed? Or "Irishman"? Or "Buddhist?" The tree, the city, and the taxi driver exist in reality, but you, you have a distinct mental representation of them: the proof is that it subsists in you, even when you are locked up in a dark room, even when you are sleeping.

By the same token, it can be said that a brand is a mental representation, and that it is also a social representation in the sense that it is formed both through direct personal interaction with a brand, and through indirect interaction via each individual's sociocultural environment.

From there, we can obviously apply to brands the functional schemas that specialists have ascribed to social representations, and, for example, use the idea of "central core" developed, as we said earlier, by authors like J. C. Abric. This central core, which has become "core identity," is of immense help to psychologists and sociologists: it makes it possible for them to untangle the interminable lists of identity components that they have to deal with in order to describe the complexity of such a concept. They manage this by distinguishing on the one hand that which is "essential" (in the core) and on the other that which is less so (on the periphery).

Let us note that neurology uses very similar images: A. Damasio, for example, makes a distinction between what he calls "core consciousness" and "extended consciousness." The first is "a simple, biological phenomenon; it has one single level of organization; it is stable across the lifetime of the organism," while the second is a complex biological phenomenon with multiple levels of organization.[7]

It thus seems that quite a few specialists agree on this point: individual and collective representations are organized in concentric circles, with a core at the center and, around this core, a periphery.

Duly noted.

But can we somehow escape this way of looking at things?

Maybe—in any case, my intention is to find an escape route, for all of the reasons that I mentioned above: the desire to avoid dualism whenever possible, to avoid the temptation to cut the world in two, to reduce the riches of life to a primitive opposition between interior and exterior, inside and outside, mind and body. It is this division that is at work behind the conception of brand identity that currently prevails: essence, or the essential, is supposed to be located in one's "core identity", while the rest is located outside this core. A part of the brand, the most invisible and impalpable part, is supposedly the most precious, the most "noble," while the rest is contingent, and doesn't belong in the magic circle of identity.

I refuse to transpose to brands this relic of Manichean thinking. Both my experience as a consumer and my professional practice militate against that type of thinking. Identity is everywhere, even in the brand's smallest elements, and in what can be concretely perceived just as much as in its invisible "values".

What's more, when one looks at things from the point of view of complex thought, or complexity science, it is difficult to be satisfied with a way of reasoning that only knows how to count to two. The physicist J.-M. Levy-Leblond wrote an entire book[8] in order to demonstrate the scientific invalidity of various binary oppositions, for example true/false, straight/curved, constant/variable, real/fictional, and so on.

So when it comes to brand identity, how can we get rid of that core/periphery dictatorship? First of all by ceasing to imagine a core as something that is necessarily homogeneous, stable, and dense.

But also by claiming the right to evoke other images.

FOUR MODELS OF IDENTITY

There are indeed other models, other ways of "picturing" something, even something as abstract as identity and as complex as a brand—if we agree that a brand is something that can be pictured.

In fact, there are at least four.[9]

The first model is the one that, as we have seen, utterly dominates depictions of brand identity: the ***atom***, a simple and very attractive image in that it makes it possible to associate a symbol of modern science, the idea of tremendous power, with the idea of maximum returns, as certain advertising specialists know very well.[10]

The second model "could be derived from biology, and notably from the phenomenon of ***coagulation***, in which elements that are normally scattered in the blood are brought together and combined."[11]

The third model is the ***tapestry*** or mosaic model.

The fourth is "based on astronomical observations, and reveals our psychological processes along with the ***constellations***, which, in spite of being virtual, are reference points all the same (for navigation, for example)".[12]

Let us take this last model: no more core, just points. If we draw a line from one point to another, a design appears, depicting an object (the Great Chariot), or, if one prefers, an animal (Ursa Major). But if we link all of the points together, we no longer get an outline. We get a network.

Now, let's move one of the nodal points of the network—up, to the left, any which way: the others move, too, more or less. If we enlarge one or two of the nodal points, and shrink one of their neighbors, the ties that bind them move in turn. Let's arbitrarily change the size and the position of the nodal points, the length, the thickness and the tension of their bonds, slowly here, and faster over there.

We get a much more accurate image of identity.

Why? Because it is more like a trace, an impression, a fingerprint—but a living, breathing one:

- like a fingerprint, it has a general outline, a contour, a motif that is either sharp or blurred, regular or misshapen, but that is always recognizable, just like the footprints of a bird walking in the wet sand;

- like a living organism, it has mobility, flexibility, and is capable of change, of being versatile.

When brand identity is likened to a human being, I don't know where the center, the core of this human being is, and I have no reason for choosing among the various prefabricated ways of thinking that would have me situate it either in the head, the heart, the body, or the "soul," whatever the latter word may mean to you.

I have no other choice but to think of the human being as a whole and to think that its identity also forms a whole.

Transposed to brands, it seems to follow that this whole is an undifferentiated blur—yet, to the contrary, its structure is very precise, as we'll see in the second part of this book.

But this means at least one thing, which is that nothing requires us to adhere to the "core identity" ideology, even less so if it takes the form of the famous "hard core" that the business world likes so much. Brand identity isn't enclosed in any hard core. To claim that it is means regressing to an archaic mode of thinking. "The hard core of a doctrine," writes Edgar Morin, "in its obviousness and its coherence, looks like an absolute rationality, when in fact this rationality is rationalization."[13]

And I would add: rationalism, as well—which, as we know, has little in common with reason.

SOMEWHERE BETWEEN ORDER AND DISORDER—WHERE DOES BRAND IDENTITY BELONG?

You may have had the experience of recognizing a face while flipping through an old family album, and of having been able to recognize it over the course of several pages. First a little girl, standing near a chair with a hoop and a sailor's costume. Someone wrote under the photo: "Louise, summer 1923." Then a young woman on her wedding day, in a woman's suit with square shoulders, as the fashion of the 1940s would have it. And so on. Each time, you recognize Louise. She has no special distinguishing features, no wart on the side of her chin, no crooked teeth, nothing remarkable at all. She is neither ugly nor pretty, and she changes a bit over time. And yet, there can be no doubt: in spite of the changes in hairstyle and fashion, it's the same person you see growing, changing, aging from page to page, over sixty or seventy years. Even if you don't know anything about her life, you can see it's her, because you recognize her even when there are several other people in the photo.

Can it be said that the little girl with the hoop and the old lady in black in the last photo are one and the same person—Louise, at the beginning and at the end of her life?

The answer is obviously yes, and obviously no. We can only think about life and living things in a complex way, and this complex way of thinking isn't taken in by binary opposition: it knows that a thing and its opposite can be true at the same time.

If we think of brands as persons, we have to accept that this is one of the rules of the game, and apply it to identity.

But once we do that, a major difficulty arises: one consequence of this complex way of approaching the problem is to seriously undermine the dogma of coherence, which is so deeply anchored in brand logic. What should we do when on the one hand, coherence seems so vital for the brand's life, while on the other it is opposed to the contradictions inherent to the complexity of living things?

Once again, we must leave dualism behind. The choice is not one between order and disorder, coherence and incoherence, law and anarchy: complexity is not opposed to simplicity, rather it includes both the simple and the complex, the coherent and the incoherent, order and disorder. It says that the two terms of any opposition are present together in life, which mutilates and destroys itself whenever it tries to choose one at the expense of the other.

Intuitively, everyone senses that the logic of life is contradictory. But when it's a matter of drawing on that logic in order to come up with rules to live by on a daily basis, well, that's a different story.

And yet, these rules exist.

Here's one: we know that for information theory, everything that hinders the correct transfer of a message X from point A to point B is called "noise." The worker who absentmindedly reverses one of the eight pieces of a poster in a subway station, making it impossible to read the price of a "Halloween Special" hamburger, causes "noise." Or take the person who, forgetting that the tops of the seats along the platform would hide it from view, came up with another poster, also for the subway, which displays the brand name on the bottom—he also causes "noise." Marketing carefully hunts down all such "noise," and in this quest it remains faithful to Shannon, whose goal was to eliminate all of the parasites capable of garbling a message, so as to reduce transmission costs.

However, the theoreticians of complexity have a different approach: for them, there is no "good" (the absence of noise = a message that has been transmitted correctly, a well-oiled machine) and "evil" (a disruptive noise = wrench in the works). Noise can become something "good," can acquire meaning and value.

It is worth citing the work and theories of several of these theoreticians:

- biophysicist H. von Foerster's 1959 theory of "order form noise";

- biologist H. Atlan's "complexity from noise" theory;[14]

- anthropologist G. Balandier's idea of disorder as a "creator of order";[15]

■ chemist I. Prigogine's the "dissipative structures" (Prigogine was awarded the Nobel Prize in 1977 for his contributions to non-equilibrium thermodynamics).

In the world of brands, it often happens that some kind of "noise" or "disorder" interrupts routine and is at first perceived as a serious disruption: we need only think of the accidents that, converted into fortuitous pieces of luck, gave birth to Ivory soap or to Kellogg's cornflakes. And how many big advertising campaigns are also born from creative ideas that were initially rejected as too extravagant or disturbing?

Marketing is a control freak that always prefers order to disorder, an indispensable quality when you're an accountant, which is exactly what marketing is, since it was born in the accounting and management divisions of the first big assembly-line companies. But the accounting mentality becomes a handicap when creativity is needed, especially in an era in which no brand can survive without constantly innovating. Now, innovation always begins by introducing an element of disorder into the order of things, and, first of all, into the order of mentalities.

It follows that marketing, despite the way it has held brands at gunpoint, is not the discipline best-suited to deal with innovation.

In any case, it's certainly not the only one.

THE ARCHITECTURE OF LIVING SYSTEMS COMES TO THE RESCUE OF BRAND IDENTITY

Three scientists from different backgrounds can help us to change perspective.

The first is Antoine Danchin, the Director of the Department of Biochemistry and Molecular Genetics at the Pasteur Institute in Paris. He was trained as a mathematician and took part in a seminar led by C. Lévi-Strauss in 1975, the proceedings of which were published under the title *Identity*, a book that I've already had occasion to cite.

In 1998, he published a book entitled *The Delphic Boat*.[16]

The title alludes to a well-known riddle often used by classical philosophy, a question asked to the Delphic oracle that directly concerns identity:

If we consider for example a boat made of planks, what is it that makes the boat a boat? This question is more than just a mind game: as time passes, some of the planks start to rot and have to be replaced. There comes a time when not one of the original planks is left. The boat still looks like the original one, but in material terms it has changed. Is it still the *same* boat?

The answer is yes, because:

> What is important about the material of the planks, apart from their relative stability over time, is the fact that it allows them to be shaped, so that they relate to one another in a certain way.

In other words, examining the planks to see if they're made of oak or pine isn't all that useful: "the boat is the *relationship* between the planks." The same is true for living organisms, and that is why "the study of life should never be restricted to objects, but must look into their relationships."

If we seek to transpose this principle to marketing—and a thousand apologies are due to A. Danchin for this unauthorized transfer—we would say that the elements of the marketing mix do not in the least describe how the brand functions, or better yet (or worse): the more we analyze in great detail one of those elements, the further we get from the conditions necessary for understanding how the whole functions. Just as the nature of the planks (oak or pine) is of little importance for the Delphic boat's enduring identity, a product's content (are there anti-free radicals or vitamin C in a hydrating cream?) or the content of some instance of communication (humorous or serious?) is not what's most important for maintaining brand identity. What really counts is the structure of relationships among the elements in the marketing mix, as well as the structure of the relationships between the marketing mix and the consumer.

The second scientist I would now like to mention works along similar lines: Antonio Damasio, world-famous neurologist and the author of *Descartes' Error: Emotion, Reason, and the Human Brain*,[17] which helped many professionals change their vision of what it means to be human, including where identity is concerned. In his first book, he began with an astonishing case study involving one Phineas Gage, who in 1848 was the victim of a workplace accident in which a five-foot iron bar weighing thirteen pounds passed through his skull. To everyone's surprise, Phineas survived. Two months later, completely healed despite the loss of his left eye, he went back to work, but it was then that it was discovered that, as Damasio writes, "Gage was no longer Gage." His body was still alive, but someone else was inhabiting it, someone neither his colleagues nor his family recognized. This someone possessed all the faculties of attention, perception, memory, language, and intelligence. He thus seemed in full possession of his reason, and yet, his behavior was becoming so odd that he lost all of the jobs he found, one after another, led a more and more chaotic life for ten or so years, and ended up dying of a series of epileptic fits in San Francisco, in 1861.

Other similar cases studied by Damasio brought him to a clear conclusion: contrary to what his training had led him to believe, emotions are not a disruptive horde laying siege to the fortress of reason. Or, to use the terminology of information theory, emotions are not "noise" that hinders the rational mechanism and prevents it from working properly: without them, that mechanism would break down. That's what happened to Phineas Gage: his "emotional" brain had been destroyed by the accident, preventing him from behaving normally. In other words, for a human being to be and remain what he is, he needs both a body (where sensations and emotions are felt) and a mind.

What was Descartes' error? It can be summed up entirely in his famous formula: "I think, therefore I am" which led to a categorical separation between the immaterial, ethereal mind and the material, palpable body.

Once again (and with the same apologies as before), if we transpose this to brands, it becomes obvious that marketing insisted on putting identity in the second category, the mind category—whence the "essence" theme, the circle metaphor or the image of the "core identity's" protective sphere, which encloses the precious and intangible capacity for producing ideas, knowledge, and reason.

In another book, Damasio confirms and deepens his early analyses, and he agrees with Danchin about identity:

> Although the building blocks for the construction of our organisms are regularly replaced, the architectural designs for the varied structures of our organisms are carefully maintained. [...] No component remains the same for very long, and most of the cells and tissues that constitute our bodies today are not the same we owned when we entered college. What remains the same, in good part, is the construction plan for our organism structure...[18]

This is what makes him respond to François Jacob,[19] who defines his "core identity" by referring to a "statue within."[20] "We do not have a self sculpted in stone and, like stone, resistant to the ravages of time."

That makes two researchers, then, who are in agreement that *the identity of a living organism is defined by the structure of the relationships that unify its elements, and not by those elements themselves.*

Now, what about the third?

The third says the same thing, but goes further toward describing the structure in question.

Harvard University professor of vascular biology D. Ingber, just like Damasio and Danchin, recalls that "understand what the parts of a complex machine are made of ... does little to explain how the whole system works."

Like the others, he then turns to the question of what links these various parts, to what he calls their "rules for their assembly." It seems that there is a principle of assembly that cuts transversally through every scale of living organism. From carbon atoms to the human being and other living creatures, a single architectural principle that he calls "tensegrity" governs the aforementioned "rules of assembly".[21] Tensegrity is a system's ability to stabilize itself through the play of tension and compression forces that are distributed through the system and lend it balance.

Ingber also reaffirms that the elements that compose the organism are constantly renewed, and that it is the enduring nature of their architecture that characterizes life.

For Ingber, the principle of tensegrity is what explains the stabilization of living structures, and not the existence of a dense, fixed "core". When Ingber models a cell subjected to tensegrity, we see that the core is not represented by a sphere but by a little grouping of stems inside a bigger grouping, like a little bird's cage inside a bigger one, and what's more a cage with a mobile shape: the core—the little cage—moves and is shaped along with the big one.

Let us note that "the tension on one of the elements is transmitted to all the other elements in the structure, including the most distant ones", as is the rule in systems theory.

What can we conclude from this for the question of brand identity?

That once again, brand identity is based less on the existence of a "core identity" whose "content" could be defined, than on a relational structure.

That this structure is composed of a network of bonds (stems, cables, or tubes) arranged according to motifs like "spirals, pentagons, or triangular forms." And that it is this balance between "bonds in tension" and "bonds in compression" that ensures the cohesion of the whole, even making it possible for that whole to change shape under the impact of a force applied to a specific point in the network without coming undone or breaking apart. If there are "cores" or rather "nodal points," they are found at the junction of the stems or bonds. Thus, it's what circulates among them (and not what is found within them) that determines the structure's integrity and thus the identity of the whole. This idea is at opposite poles from the military-like fortress that we usually and wrongly imagine when we talk about brand identity.

KEY POINTS

- The notion of identity, and its extension to qualitative marketing, brand identity, is neither fixed, nor rigid, nor "inscribed" in the manner of DNA.

- This analogy with the genetic code is reductive and deceptive and constitutes a dangerous reference point for brand management.

- The nature of brand identity is hybrid, that is to say both material and immaterial. It is impossible to untangle these two components or to privilege one over the other.

- Brand identity is not a kernel, a core, or a center; it is an open, flexible structure.

- This structure obeys the principle of tensegrity, and ensures the continuity of the brand's life by maintaining a dynamic, rather than a static, equilibrium.

PART II
An Analytical Method

CHAPTER 4

The Fingerprint Method Concept

Once the founding principles of brand identity have been redefined, it remains to put forward an analytical method that makes it possible to both identify brand identity and to manage it with the help of a simple, clear diagram: the Fingerprint Method, which was conceived to follow the creation and the evolution of the mental imprints or impressions left by brands in the public's mind.

It was a pleasant spring weekend, and we were staying in a pretty house on the coast in northern France to celebrate my father-in-law's 80th birthday. Outside, there was a garden full of roses, a bit of sunshine, two dogs, and the whole family, having a good time. My goddaughter, Caroline, who was eight years old at the time, timidly approached the desk where I had my nose in a big book, and asked:

"What are you doing?"

"I'm working," I said.

"What are you working on?"

I hesitated. How should I go about explaining my job to a little girl?

"I'm thinking about brands."

Though I'd done my best to make my answer accessible, it clearly didn't make much sense to her. I tried again:

"Do you know what a brand is?" I said, and I hastened to add: "It's like a mark."[1]

She furrowed her brow and thought for one or two seconds, then held out her arm, and said:

"Like this?"

On her forearm there was a tiny scar. I was about to say no, that wasn't the kind of mark that I was interested in, when I, too, began to think. To help her understand, I could have cited Coca-Cola or McDonald's: every kid knows about them. But if I pushed the question-and-answer session any further, I suspected I would just make things more complicated. For her, McDonald's might have been a restaurant where her parents took her after the movies, a Big Mac and fries, or her best friend's birthday party. Coca-Cola could have been what she drank from a straw at McDonald's, a soda machine at the supermarket entrance, or the name on her classmate's pencil box. So I gave up and said:

"Yes, like that."

It's not that kids are always right, but in this case I had the chance to apply a fundamental principle of communication theory: if I've told Caroline that a brand is like a mark, and if for her a mark is the little trace on her forearm, I have to begin from this point of view, and not from my own, if I want to start a discussion with her and have any chance of being understood. Her perception of things prevails: she is necessarily right because she can't help seeing things the way she does.

Kids aren't always right, but sometimes they do help us get back to what's essential. And there was something essential about Caroline's response. If we examine this response closely, what do we find?

First, that a brand is a mark or a trace. Which means that it tells a story, one that is known or unknown, ancient or recent. For there to be a trace, time—even a short period—must have passed. A brand's *temporal* dimension is impossible to ignore.

Next, a trace is a legible sign, it has material reality. The story that it tells may be intangible, but a scar on the skin, a footprint in the sand, a notch in a piece of wood—these are all concrete things. A brand's *physical* dimension is equally impossible to ignore.

Finally, the trace is located in a particular place: if we move it, it won't mean the same thing any longer. A scar makes it possible to recognize someone because it is located in one spot and not in another. If it is found elsewhere than where we saw it the first time, this suggests that we're dealing with someone else. A brand's *spatial* dimension is impossible to ignore.

These are three dimensions to be taken into account, three essential components of brands, as we'll see. There are others.

Caroline is my goddaughter and I am her godmother. But it must be added that I'm a horrible godmother, a fact that has several consequences for the rest of my demonstration:

First consequence: in my relationship with her, I fail to respect the current *norms*, I don't do any of the things that one is supposed to do in order to be a "good" godmother. As she gets older, she realizes this: she has a godfather, she has a sister and friends who have godmothers and godfathers who behave "as they're supposed to." The game has unspoken rules, she knows them, and I don't apply them.

Second consequence: in addition to being her godmother, I'm her Uncle Pierre's wife. But she doesn't see Uncle Pierre very often, and besides him, she knows nothing about me. She doesn't know where I was born, where I grew up, what I like, or what I do, how I live. What's more, she has no idea what I'm planning to do tomorrow, in three months, or next year. Since she isn't familiar with my intentions, my desires, my *projects*, she can't form any idea of who I am.

Third consequence: she lives in Switzerland, and I in Paris. We see each other for a few hours every year at family reunions. The quality of our *relations* suffers from this: they're affectionate but superficial, weak, and with lots of spaces in between visits.

Fourth consequence: I'm an adult, she's a child. Our reciprocal *positions* are very different. Even without being her godmother, I've lived through more than she has and know more than she does—or, at least, I've lived through and know different things. In any event, for the moment, that gives me various advantages (or various burdens): freedom, maturity, experience, knowledge.

As I said above, the relations between brands and consumers are not identical to the relations established between two people. So I'm going to let Caroline go back outside and rejoin her dog, her sister, and her cousins, without pushing the comparison any further.

But this little anecdote has enabled me to address four other components of brands. A brand

- is defined with respect to certain *norms* explicitly or implicitly present in its environment;

- proposes and defines *projects*;

- brings two *positions* face to face;

- is focused around certain kinds of *relations*.

Four components, plus the three I mentioned earlier, equals seven in total. This number has a magical air about it, and may therefore arouse our suspicions, but I assure you that there's nothing supernatural going on here, nor anything arbitrary or even intuitive: these seven components are the result of recent researches in communication theory.

WHY SEVEN CONTEXTS?

Let's remember why, when confronted with a marketing concept (brand identity), it's not from marketing but from communication theory that we can get some fresh air and serious thinking.

It's quite simple: everything, in life, is not about marketing, whereas if it is true that "One cannot not communicate" (and to this day, we're still waiting for someone to prove it wrong), it follows that "Everything is communication". Of course, the kind of communication we're dealing with, here, has nothing to do with marketing. Communication theory is interested about human communication. Marketing uses that word in a much more narrow and technical sense, meaning advertising, promotion, PR, sponsoring, events, etc. In other words, marketing still tends to see communication as the last quarter or the marketing-mix, a tool which alarmingly looks like a production line ending with the wrapping department.

That taylorist division of labour is everything complexity science and communication theory fight against, and this book tries to follow their path. That's why the starting point for the Fingerprint Method is not communication as marketing sees it, but as intended by communication theorists.

These theorists are scientists, and scientists usually stay away from magical numbers like thirteen or seven. So why do they claim that there are seven components in all communication processes – a brand being considered here no more nor less than one of them?

In 1956 an article called "The Magical Seven, Plus or Minus Two: Some Limits on Our Capacity for Processing Information" was published in *The Psychological Review*.[2] The author of the article was George Miller, a psychologist who declared that he was "persecuted by an integer. For seven years this number has followed me around, has intruded in my most private data, and has assaulted me from the pages of our most public journals." More seriously, Miller demonstrated that human beings have trouble distinguishing objects, phenomena, and stimuli from one another, recalling certain items, and evaluating number correctly beyond the threshold of seven. Beneath this threshold, they're able to perform many of these mental tasks, but once that threshold is crossed, they are much more likely to fail.[3]

Perhaps this phenomenon, which has been confirmed by cognitive science, justifies the existence of the seven "contexts" of communication? The fact is that "Communication theory considers that every situation can be broken down into layered contexts. Basing their conclusions on a body of work carried out by numerous specialists, the theoreticians have defined seven fundamental contexts."[4]

Here they are:

■ the physical and sensorial context;

■ the spatial context;

■ the temporal context;

■ the context of the actors' respective positioning;

■ the immediate social relations context, relative to the quality of the relations among the actors;

■ the cultural context of collective norms and rules;

■ the context of the actors' identities.

To the extent that these seven contexts are relevant in all communication situations, they are (with a few nuances or simplifications) valid for brands as well.

The first nuance concerns the word "positioning", which has a different meaning in marketing. So as not to create confusion, I will speak instead of *positions*. The second nuance will consist in shortening the expression "the immediate social relationship context, relative to the quality of the relations among the actors" and in speaking instead simply of "relations".

The third will consist, likewise, in speaking in abridged fashion of "norms."

Finally, the formula "context of identities," which denotes "what is known or what is displayed about the intentions of the actors" like a plan, an intention, or else "values, a vision, stakes," has been replaced, for simplicity's sake, by "projects."

——But before examining each of these contexts, a few clarifications are in order.

A "NON-CENTERED" NETWORK

In order to escape the centralism that depicts brands as having a core, as we saw in the first part, there are two solutions: either we decide that there's no core at all, or else that there are several. How to choose? Going back in time a little should help.

It was in the nineteenth century that the word "network" was applied for the first time to a group of communication pathways (railways, rivers, roads). If you want to get an idea of how networks were imagined at that time, look at a railway map of France or Great Britain: everything converges on a "center"—which is in fact rather decentered, toward the top or the bottom of the country, Paris or London—and radiates outward from it.

It just isn't possible to enter the third millennium with mental images that date from the Victorian period. If we've come far enough to imagine a form of network intelligence[5], the network in question most certainly does not take the form of a star radiating outward from a central hub, but rather of a net that envelops the entire planet.

—— Indeed, the most widespread image of a network today is a spider's web, thanks to the worldwide web. It no longer has any center at all; or, rather, there are billions of centers, some tiny, some gigantic, which are always on the move, growing larger or smaller, dissolving and recomposing. And all of them take part in the life of the network, in a galaxy, as Philippe Breton puts it, one that is "diffuse, spread out, and non-centered."[6]

A net can take various forms, from the simplest (a hammock or a fishing net) to the most complicated. Ask your grandmother, the specialist of crocheted tea cozies: she'll explain to you that there are dozens of usable "points," each with a different motif, and all of them capable of being combined with the others.

Each of us can choose his or her motif. Mine, for the reasons that I have laid out, has seven "points" or poles. To show that they are interconnected, I have organized them not in the form of a list, but in a geometrical figure with seven poles, which is explained and diagrammed in Figure 2.

And if I prefer to speak of poles rather than cores, this is because a core is hard, closed, stable, and compact, whereas these poles are not. These are not the tightly-woven knots of a fishing net. These are open, mobile places, virtual crossroads, places of exchange and transit, points of concentration but also of circulation. A pole has no precise contours, and this imprecision is suited to the logic of a living system.

Moreover, a pole is a magnetic field: it attracts and displaces, it produces movement, is a dynamic factor. This, too, is what makes living things alive.

TO MANIPULATE OR TO ACTIVATE? THAT IS THE QUESTION

The "Fingerprint Method" that I am proposing here consists in manipulating one or several of the seven poles of communication. Sometimes I'll say manipulate, and sometimes I'll speak of "activating" such and such a pole.

In order to avoid all misunderstanding, let me specify: for me, the word "manipulate" is neutral.

To think the opposite, and to get indignant because marketing and advertising "manipulate" consumers is at once to give them too much credit and to reason in a way that's been outdated for forty years. It's to place oneself back in the era of V. Packard and *The Hidden Persuaders* (1957), likening the relationship between brands and the public to the big bad wolf pulling a fast one on Little Red Riding Hood.

Those days are over. It still happens that marketing hazards some more or less rudimentary stratagem in the unacknowledged hope of tricking the consumer—and, sometimes, these stratagems even work. But this is increasingly rare, because consumers have changed over the last twenty or thirty years. Today's consumer is infinitely less naïve, more skilled, and more opportunistic. Marketing itself has formed (or deformed) the consumer, and in any case has immunized him: can we still speak of manipulation when the public knows all of the magician's tricks? That doesn't prevent us from applauding, even in all sincerity, but in the way a connoisseur admires an artist's talent, and not because we believe there's really some kind of magic going on. Most of the time, the consumers give as good as they get. They manipulate brands as much as they are manipulated by them.

In any event, on this subject, I'll simply highlight P. Watzlawick's position:

> Today *any* form of influence, in particular anything that can be labeled as manipulation, is attacked and condemned as being unethical. These attacks are not merely directed at the abuses of manipulation—which, needless to say, are always possible—but to manipulation as such. Their origin seems to be the blind, utopian belief that human existence is […] possible without any mutual influence whatsoever… […] I shall merely summarize here: one cannot *not* influence. It is, therefore, absurd to ask how influence and manipulation can be avoided, and we are left with the inescapable responsibility of deciding for ourselves how this basic law of human communication may be obeyed in the most humane, ethical, and effective manner.[7]

This is, as usual with Watzlawick, an eminently pragmatic position, with a variation on the well-known theme of "One cannot *not* communicate." Communicating always means trying to influence others. Our only choice is between doing it well and doing it badly—not doing it at all simply isn't an option. And so, without getting all worked up about it, I'll speak of manipulating the seven poles of communication, much as one says that an osteopath manipulates a patient's spinal column, or that a surgeon manipulates his surgical instruments—in the sense of handling, performing an action.

SEVEN POLES, SEVEN HOLOGRAMS

Each of the seven poles can refer to all the others: all of them are linked. If a brand is a system, its functioning is "hologramic," fractal: the smallest of the brand's elements contains the entire brand, says something about it, and sends the message in all directions in real time. A sticker that's half an inch off center, stuck on an envelope that's part of a mass mailing, can, all by itself, put a brand's image in danger—even a brand that is conscientious, venerable, and nice, and convinced that keeping up its client data base is of capital importance for its survival.

Let's imagine that Mrs. Miller, whose acquaintance we made at the beginning of this book, and who has been ordering clothes from the 3 Suisses mail-order catalogue for thirty years, receives some mail one day. It's November, and for once Mrs. Miller hasn't ordered anything since the end of the summer, despite having received some flyers with special offers and being offered free gifts in the last catalogue. But in the most recent of these mailings, Mrs. Miller sees an announcement, "25 % off EVERYTHING!", as well as a little sticker that reads: "Please note, unless we hear from you about this promotional offer, we will unfortunately be unable to send you our next catalogue."

What! Mrs. Miller says to herself, I've been ordering clothes two or three times a year for the whole family for thirty years, and just because I haven't bought anything this time, they're not going to send me the next catalogue? Do they really think I'm going to put up with this kind of blackmail? Or that I can't buy the catalogue myself, if I feel like it? Or that they can make me do what they want just by giving me a mean look, as if I were a little schoolgirl?

Mrs. Miller is angry. How angry, we don't know, nor whether her anger will prevent her from ordering from 3 Suisses again. But in any event, anger of this kind leaves a trace, an impression. In this case, the trace went from the "Physical" pole (a little golden sticker stuck diagonally to the envelope of a mass mailing) to the "Relations" pole (I liked them, they're treating me badly), from there to the "Norms" pole (it simply isn't done to speak in that tone to a good client), jumped to the "Temporal" pole (thirty years of loyalty for nothing?), and then on to the "Positions" pole (I'm not a child whom one threatens with punishment if she doesn't behave "properly") and the "Projects" pole (if they're going to treat me like that, I'm never going to order from them again).

Of course, we can guess what led the brand to put the sticker on all of the November mail addressed to clients who hadn't yet ordered anything: the 3 Suisses[8] catalogue is expensive, and it would be a waste to send it to someone if they weren't going to use it. But that's the way the company thinks, and the company isn't the brand. If 3 Suisses had decided to approach the issue from an ecological angle, they could easily have made the sticker part of an anti-waste campaign, which would have given it a different meaning. Instead, the sticker reveals a purely cold and calculating business strategy. The result? Mrs. Miller is immediately repositioned as just any old consumer—or, worse still, as a mistreated one. And when someone tries to tell her what to do, she plays hardball. A minor incident, you'll say. But multiplied by how many clients likely to react the way Mrs. Miller did?

Brand identity works as a network organized around the seven poles, each of them linked to all the others, and the slightest pressure applied to one is inevitably transmitted, with greater or lesser strength, to the whole network.

NO COMMUNICATION OUT OF CONTEXT

There is no communication out of context. Only scientific utterances—though not all of them—can claim to be *context free*, in other words detached from the conditions of their elaboration: "2 plus 2 equals four," or "the net upward buoyancy force is equal to the magnitude of the weight of fluid displaced by the body."

In the humanities, the opposite is the case: without a context, an utterance has no meaning, whether it's as sophisticated as the thought of Wittgenstein or as simple as the expression "See you Tuesday." For according to whether I say "See you Tuesday" to my friends at the bridge club or to the doctor who is going to give me the results of my biopsy, the same words obviously don't have the same meaning.

In the world of brands, there has recently been a lot of talk about meaning.[9] There has been a call "for meaning," a call for "content," sometimes with the implication that the one implies the other, and that wherever there's content, meaning is sure to follow. The avalanche of books, articles, seminars, conferences, and consultancies devoted to Brand Content attests to the phenomenon.[10]

But it's not enough to inject a message with meaning for it to actually be there, much less understood. The meaning of a communication is not the exclusive property of the sender, nor is it in the message's content: it is born (or not) of the context in which the message arrives at its destination.

That's why the examination of contexts is fundamental: that's where meaning comes from—when it comes.

Hutchinson, a venerable French brand founded by an American in 1853, makes rubber and synthetic polymer products, notably for the auto industry. In 2012, its logo was framed by a triangle, and to the untrained eye, looked vaguely like a vacuum cleaner tube rolled up into a knot, the kind of thing that drives the cleaning lady mad. One must be an excellent connoisseur of the history of European companies to know that in reality the vacuum cleaner tube is a stylized eagle, and that this eagle was originally the one on the American flag. Such a symbol has long since lost its meaning for a company that is still French. But even supposing that instead of the eagle, one sees a tube, this tube would only have meaning with respect to a former activity (making tires), which today occupies a very small place in Hutchinson's line of products. The signification of the logo has been considerably blurred, to the point that it is only accessible by means of a historical reconstruction. The initial context has been lost, and with it, the previous meaning of the logo.

This also explains why most tests that brands undergo are artificial, difficult to interpret, and sometimes completely erroneous: they disconnect the object from its context, the logo from the product, the product from the packaging, the packaging from shelf space, shelf space from signage, and signage from the street or the shopping mall. But for a consumer, a tube of Lancôme lipstick doesn't have the same value when chosen with the help of a good salesperson at Saks Fifth Avenue in New York as it does when chosen for lack of anything better to do at four in the morning at the duty free shop in the Mombasa airport. Blind tests confirm this *a contrario*: perceptions change, sometimes completely, when a product is artificially detached from its brand name and its usual context of consumption.

If meaning isn't provided by the sender of a message or ingrained in some assemblage of words, forms, or images, but rather built within the contexts where the message takes place, we have to work with those concepts in order for meaning to emerge. And it has to emerge, because meaning is the key that gives access to the consumer's mind. What looks meaningless to the consumer never even makes it through to his or her consciousness.

The best way of doing this? Make it so that the key—in other words, the meaning—is provided by the consumer him or herself.

If the consumer feels like he has not only understood but discovered something, he gets hooked, once and for all.

You may be familiar with so-called random reward conditioning experiments, which consist in giving the "subjects" (this is the word that psychology uses to designate people who participate in an experiment—and it's clearly not a neutral one) a list of pairs of numbers without any connection between them. The experimenter asks them to figure out why these numbers have been paired, and the experimenter's mission is to respond "true" or "false," first infrequently, and then more and more frequently.

This leads the subject to imagine that he is dealing with a trial-and-error experiment, and that he therefore has no choice but to begin by agreeing or disagreeing at random. At first, he's wrong every time, but his performance gradually improves, and the experimenter's number of "True" responses increases. The subject arrives at a hypothesis that, even if it's not quite perfect, proves more and more reliable.

The result is that the hypothesis becomes a certainty, and the subject soon adopts it as a self-evident truth, refusing to give it up even when the experimenter tells him or her that the "True" and "False" responses were completely arbitrary. Some of the subjects even seem to think that they've discovered some underlying pattern that experimenter himself wasn't aware of.[11]

This confirms that meaning is not in the object that is being observed but rather is built by the reasoning or perceptions of the observer. In and of itself, "reality" has no meaning (a credit card has no meaning "in itself", and someone who had never seen one before could just as well try to eat it or use it to plug a hole as hang it around his neck for decorative effect). What's more, this meaning is all the more credible and powerful for having been "discovered" by the observer. No advertisement had as much effect on Frau Schneider's husband, a doctor from Hamburg, as the experience of driving a Smart while his Mercedes was under repair: he was able to see for himself that it was just as fast and easy to drive around in a Smart as in a Mercedes, and today he would rather "look like a clown," as he says, than waste hours looking for a parking spot. During the week, his Mercedes no longer leaves the garage.

This clarifies matters: since meaning is the key to the consumer's consciousness (and thus makes it possible to gain access to his or her interest, attention, confidence, patronage, even loyalty, that is to say to all the criteria for a brand's effectiveness), and since it is born in context, we have to work on and influence the context.

KEY POINTS

- The Fingerprint Method is organized around seven poles.

- These seven poles are linked together and interactive: they form a system of communication.

- They form a non-centered network that is constantly (slowly or quickly, visibly or invisibly) being reconfigured. Each pole should be viewed not as a knot or a core, but as a hub, an intersection where all of the internal and external information about the brand is dispatched and transferred.

■ Brand identity is the structure that is created by the poles that are most frequently used by the brand.

■ When the connections among the seven poles are traced, a design appears that represents brand identity.

FIGURE 2 ▏The Fingerprint Method

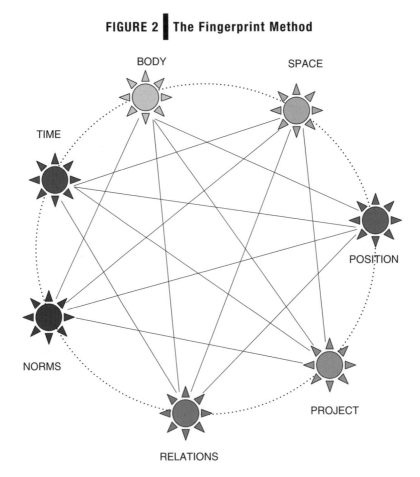

CHAPTER 5

The Fingerprint Method: The Seven Poles

Everything that makes up a brand is a process of communication: product design, pricing and distribution, reliability of services, advertising, the way salespeople look, the way clients look, the logo, the product's history, shopping bags, stickers, the color of the carpet in stores—everything. Communication permeates the totality of the Brand system.

Looking at things from this angle makes it possible to gain perspective on the marketing mix. The latter is typically subdivided into four sections, and brands often use the same diagram, which takes into account the product, its price, place, and promotion, which used to be called the 4 P's. Some authors have added other "P's", at the cost of some linguistic gymnastics, without truly managing to dethrone the initial model, which is probably unshakeable because of the symbolic value of the number 4, a very ancient symbol of totality.

In this diagram, promotion (which today has been rechristened "communication") is but a link in the chain, and the last one at that: it's completely subordinated to the others.

For communication theory, which looks at things in a much wider frame, no such subordination is possible: as we have seen, everything is communication. There is also no such thing as a reasoning process linking elements together in linear fashion, nothing like a straightforward montage. Applied to brands, this means distributing its component parts in accordance with a completely different logic: instead of lining them up one after another, they are distributed around the seven poles.

Thus the first link in the chain, the "product," can be found attached to several of these seven poles, which correspond to the seven possible contexts for a process of communication—and it should be recalled here that brands are considered globally as such a communicative process.

Let's take a Swatch watch: it can be analyzed as an object endowed with very particular characteristics, including its price (Physical context), also, of course, in the Temporal context (and not only because it's a watch, but because it's a watch that can be changed each season, in other words that is itself part of the temporal flow it measures), in the Norms context (the brand owes its success to a reversal of technical norms) as well as in the Relations context (Swatch de-dramatized and democratized watch-wearing). Ever since opening boutiques with very strong personalities, the brand is also working in the Spatial context.

The brand's identity will be more or less rich according to the number of poles in which it operates, and not as a function of time spent occupying one or another of them year after year. The jeweler "Mellerio dit Meller" may be the oldest French brand, since it goes back to the early sixteenth century, and passing the torch from generation to generation for so long is certainly an accomplishment, but it doesn't mean identity creation: outside the microcosm of Parisian jewelry, "Mellerio dit Meller" is not a brand.

This example provides an occasion for underscoring once more that a brand cannot be reduced to its legal definition. It's a collective construction: the participation of two partners is necessary, the company and the consumers in the largest sense, including those who don't buy the brand in question. The only criterion that makes it possible to say whether a brand exists is identity, which is strong or weak according to the number of activated poles. It is not possible to decree unilaterally "We are a brand," except for internal reasons. For example, Air France announced one day that it was reducing the number of its "brands" from ten to seven, keeping First Class, Business, Alizé, Tempo Challenge, Tempo, Navette, and Air France by. In truth, outside the company, none of these is considered to be a brand (except perhaps Navette, and then only for people who fly a lot). They will become brands on the day they win their independence and are able to fly under their own power, so to speak, rather than remaining hidden under the parent company's protective wing. To take a counterexample, British Airways makes it very clear that what passengers are buying is the British Airways brand, and not the "sub-brands" that are services like Club World or Euro Traveller.

There is thus no question of choosing one of the contexts and making it the basis of brand identity, in accordance with an oft-championed principle of marketing, which states that choosing one single message is the only way to make oneself stand out from the crowd. This principle has merit within the marketing mix, where it seeks to provide a rational foundation for the fourth link in the chain, namely promotion: it helps to avoid superfluous or counterproductive use of media channels.

But for the logic of communication theory, the distinction between the media and the not-media makes no sense: everything is a media. The product is a media, the price is a media, the distribution network too, and a promotional key-chain is also, just as much as a television spot.

By the same token, it is vain to keep saying just one thing in hopes of making oneself heard. Identity isn't one, it is multiple. Obviously, if it was completely fragmented, it would never coalesce: but its stability is less dependent on choosing one communicative pole (this is just about impossible in any case) than on the path that the brand regularly traces from one pole to the next.

THE PHYSICAL POLE

Why begin with the Physical pole?

Not because it's the most important, but because it corresponds to the brand's body, the one to which our five senses give immediate access. I hesitate to point out something so obvious, but without those five senses, we would know nothing about the world around us nor anything about ourselves: we quite simply wouldn't exist.

A truism? Perhaps, but when an entire society gets caught up in a virtual world, it's worth recalling that this virtual world is a fantasy. And this fantasy is at work everywhere, including in the world of brands. Think of a two-page ad by Audi calling for "Less material, more ideas" or Compaq's declaration that what's most important is not what's "under the hood" of its computers, but what's in people's minds.

It's as if the mind had no concrete foundation. As if, once again, we had to divide mind and matter, and dismiss one whenever we are dealing with the other. As if, after decades of over-the-top materialism, there was no other choice but to head in the opposite direction, toward a no less over-the-top immaterialism.

Even if our whole culture pushes us in this direction, with encouragement from technology, we must refuse this dichotomy between body and mind. Without the body, there would be no identity: there is neither means nor sufficient reason for denying this self-evident truth.

Yet the Physical pole of brand identity is not the most important one: none of the seven poles is more important than the others, which is why they are arranged in a circle, equidistant from one another. But it is an unavoidable part of any brand, including service brands, including Internet brands, which (until someone proves otherwise) are materialized at least via our screens. Some brands have understood this, such as FedEx:

Our customers [...] have a symbiotic relationship with FedEx: when they turn on their PC, one of the first things they see on the screen is FedEx. To this degree, when we say we want to get close to our customers, we don't mean it in a metaphorical way. That phrase has become a cliché because there is no physical manifestation. We *do* mean it physically.[1]

The body of the brand

What can be gathered around the Physical pole? Everything that makes up the body of the brand, in other words, every object, person, or material element that bears its name (starting with the name itself), or that represents the brand, everything that can be materially grasped or measured, everything perceivable by the five senses. For example:

- the product, of course, whether we're talking about its color, shape, or material; its taste, smell, or tactile or auditory qualities.

- its name;

- its logo;

- its graphic design;

- its price;

- its packaging;

- its wrapping;

- its jingle, if it has one;

- its merchandising

- its website, Facebook, and Twitter pages;

- the voice that answers the telephone for a call center;

- the person that handles a file (the way that person looks, dresses, speaks, answers questions, etc.) for a service brand.

As the list grows longer (and it can get even longer), we can see that what happens at the Physical pole is never strictly material; there is obvious slippage toward the Relations, Norms, and Positions poles, as we will see, and no less obvious slippage toward the Spatial and Temporal poles.

This is why the seven poles must be at once distinguished from and linked to one another. The first, the Physical pole, has a tendency to be neglected or even forgotten ever since T. Levitt diagnosed an epidemic of "marketing myopia"[2] and drew attention to the fact that a consumer looking for a box of nails is actually buying not nails but the solution to a specific problem (hanging a painting, for example). Not an object, but a beneficial advantage. This was a salutary revelation, but one which led to an equal and opposite form of excess, consisting in the belief that deep down the product has little importance, or in any case that it was better to accentuate the advantages it brings rather than its own qualities.

Coca-Cola, which remains one of the leading brands in the world,[3] never allows itself to go on selling youth, freshness, or American-ness for too long. We regularly hear its managers take a step back and proclaim: "We're selling a drink, not happiness."

In other words, Coca-Cola keeps coming back to the body (and not to the heart, mind, or soul) of its brand, which its consumers never lose track of. When asked about the identity of such and such a brand, they usually give very concrete answers: it's a drink, a perfume, coffee-makers, a newspaper, luggage, cheese.

The Innocent brand understood this so well that it wagered everything on a single ingredient, fresh fruit juice, and nothing else: no additives, no preservatives, no added sugars. This single-minded approach, which was visible on its labels, earned it the support of British consumers and numerous laurels from the economic press, all of this in less than ten years and practically without advertising.

In the eyes of consumers, for example, Timberland is a pair of yellow boots, Campbell's a white and red can of soup. Burberry is a trench coat with an unmistakable plaid lining. Michelin is tires, Levi's a pair jeans, Lacoste a polo shirt, Dyson is vacuum cleaners and hand-dryers. Starbucks is both coffee and coffee shops. St. Dupont makes high-end cigarette lighters, and despite its attempts to create a global brand (if only to compensate for the fall in lighter sales due to anti-tobacco campaigns), its diversification into the sale of pens, watches, handbags, perfume, and menswear hasn't managed to change consumers' perceptions: for them, St. Dupont has always made and continues to make high-end cigarette lighters. The body of the brand has such weight that the brand is sometimes unable to escape it.

Sometimes, it even takes deliberate advantage of this, as if it possessed a beautiful physique that could be displayed without ornament. Think of McDonald's explaining: "We make hamburgers, and we make them well" or shoes whose attributes can be summed up in a couple of words: "Geox breathes." Or Apple, when the brand can (at least temporarily) state: MacBook Air, "the thinnest laptop in the world," or Dyson, faithful to its minimalist advertising approach, when it announces the release of a new model by declaring soberly: "It does the same work as the big model, but it's a third as light."

The body of the brand can be recognized by a *color*: orange for the bank ING Direct or for Hermès, which lays claim to it from time to time in its advertising campaigns ("Indian pink, Hermès orange" in spring 2008), and of course also for the telephone company…Orange.

By the same token, Coca-Cola is red, IBM is Big Blue, Nivea is round and white against a blue background, Tiffany is a specific shade of turquoise blue, the color of its boxes, but also the blue-white of its diamonds and the silver of its jewelry.

The Body Shop is green, Bombay Sapphire is blue, Nespresso is black, and the singer Bono even launched a "brand" of a new, charitable type, called "Red," which uses the color for its partnerships with other companies to signal that a percentage of all sales will be given to the Global Fund, which helps to fight AIDS in Africa; this is the case of one of the American Express cards, or of the SLVR model of Motorola. Red is also the name of an English magazine and that of an energy drink (Red Bull). When journalists are wanting for ideas, they avoid repetitions by speaking of the "red and black" bank to evoke Société Générale.

The body of the brand can be identified by a *material*: denim for Levi's, lead glass for Swarovski, leather for Hermès, cashmere for Pringle or Ballantyne, or it can be condensed in a *shape*. The clubs that Lord Harmsworth, owner of the Perrier spring in the early twentieth century, used for his gymnastics exercises gave their inimitable shape to the famous little green bottles. Coca-Cola's bottles initially had a shape inspired by the curves of Mae West (just as those of Virgin Cola, a few decades later, would supposedly evoke those of Pamela Anderson).

Or again, the body of the brand has a *smell*. Guerlain is one of the most famous perfumers in the world (the most famous, in its own eyes), because, it is said, it is the one that has blazed the most olfactory trails, to the Orient with Shalimar, in rose with Nahema, and in sandalwood with Samsara. In any event, for a nose that's had a little training, Guerlain perfumes are (or were) easy to distinguish from the rest: legend even has it that a secret ingredient, added in infinitesimal doses, gives them this "family resemblance" that has made them stand out as distinct perfumes with a strong personality. For this reason, one cannot change a perfume's makeup and keep its name without serious consequences for the brand's identity: Lanvin experimented with this at its own expense by modifying the formula of its legendary Arpège without telling anybody.

Taste also plays a major role in the identity of some brands. Starbucks has based its identity on a story about taste: H. Schultz built his empire by introducing Americans, who were once content with drinking bland filter coffee (which the French like to call "sock juice"), to the subtleties and varieties of different flavors of coffee. Krisprolls did the same with its little half-breads toasted according to a special "double cooking" method. Guinness owes a part of its identity to the fact that it's a dark beer, and that it has a very specific taste. Lavazza, by the same token, began by creating a special mixture of coffee grounds of different origins, then roasting them until they acquired a unique taste, which was recognizable and more stable over time than that of the coffee sold in bulk in the early twentieth century. In Italy, Campari and Fernet-Branca are immediately identifiable by their bitter taste. And the famous Marmite condiment claims a taste that is so unusual that there is no alternative: you either love it or you hate it.

Other brands are recognizable by a *sound*: we need only think of the care with which Bang & Olufsen calibrated the number of decibels triggered by the "Forward" and "Stop" buttons on its VCRs, or of the acoustics of Patek Philippe's watch mechanism; or of the way ads craft their soundtracks. In France, the Leclerc supermarkets, for example, carefully chose the voices of their characters, which have remained the same for such a long time that it is easy to recognize Philip, the father's, voice, as well as those of his wife, his mother-in-law, and his friend Regis, the pain in the neck who irritates everyone, even when you turn on the radio in the middle of an advertisement.

Many boutiques now call upon "audio designers" tasked with reinforcing the brand's identity with the aid of specific musical ambiances: the London-based Sound Agency does this, for example, as does the American company Muzak, which has changed a lot since the days when it provided hundreds of stores with the same elevator music. Today, Muzak conceives the Gap's musical background differently than it does McDonald's, and the latter even more differently than what is heard in its competitor Burger King. Muzak's vice-president explains that it's a matter of trying to capture the "essence" of each brand, its "intangible identity," and even its "values." Starbucks owes part of its success to the musical choices played in its cafés, and to the CDs for sale at the counter, next to the muffins and the mugs. And Burberry puts a lot of stock in music with its Burberry Acoustics program.

It seems more difficult for a brand to base even a part of its identity on the sense of *touch*.

And yet that is what Vaseline attempts to do in Great Britain,[4] and Ariel Sensitive, too, whose English ad campaigns play with the meaning of the word "gentle," with images in which the packshot plays a minor role at the bottom of the ad, while most of the space is taken up by depictions of the pleasure to be had by young and old from cozying up in soft textiles.[5] And while launching the iPhone, Steve Jobs didn't miss the opportunity to stress that this new telephone went so far as to make even the simplest tactile experiences into something completely innovative: "When we are born, we all receive an extremely efficient pointing system: our fingers. The iPhone uses them to create the most revolutionary user interface since the mouse." And indeed, the iPhone's users all experienced sensations they had never felt before while typing on the keyboard of their previous cell phones. The same experienced was transposed to the iPad, and has been imitated by many of Apple's competitors.

Some brands try to combine several senses at once: Hermès dedicated its creativity, artisanship, and love for objects of quality to satisfying three of the five senses: sight, smell, and touch. And it is quite true that the color orange, the Hermès scents, and the quality of the leather greatly contribute to the brand's "signature" in the eyes of its devotees—as for the rest, they are exposed only to the visual signature of color via the handbags and some ad campaigns.

In certain cases, the body of the brand is a *gesture*: Actimel began by presenting itself as "the new gesture of health in the morning." Orangina, which belongs to the Schweppes group, added a gesture (shaking up the drink) to the other specific signs that make up its brand identity, namely the product itself, its bottle, and its advertising saga. And in addition to a finger sliding across the screen, Apple added other gestures—pinching, displacing, sweeping away—that remain associated with the brand even after its competitors have adopted them in turn.

In any event, it can be seen that what first comes to mind when people are asked about such and such a brand is something material: an object, a shape, a color, a taste.

Brand identity is corporeal.

What's in a name?

The first component of identity, of course, is the name, to such a degree that many specialists think the one equals the other. This implies that changing your name means changing identity, and vice versa—and thus it's a risky and potentially dangerous enterprise. Twix is not Raider, nor are M & M's the same thing as Treets, even if it's exactly the same product.

Such a change can be extremely beneficial: Metro Sportswear didn't mean much of anything, but when re-baptized Canada Goose, this brand of ultra-cozy down jackets acquired a strong, clear, and extremely competitive identity.

But while visual identity can evolve on a regular basis without leading to any spectacular upheavals, the name carries with it such precious value that there has to be an extremely good reason for changing it.

Because of the high concentration of companies in all industry and service sectors, names changes have become very frequent of late. The companies' reasons are one thing—the consequences for brand identity, which depends on the public's acceptance and interpretation of the new name, are quite another. From this point of view, the motives and internal reversals that led Société Générale d'Entreprises to change its name to Vinci or Andersen Consulting to call itself Accenture are of little importance—all that counts is the meaning clients do or do not give to the change.

And it's better that way, because in most cases these names are themselves meaningless, whatever those who chose them may say.

Nothing in the name Vinci indicates that it's a European group specializing in concessions and construction: at first glance, one would be more likely to situate it in the cultural sector. Industrial brands, which are unaccustomed to coming into contact with the larger public, are adept at choosing esoteric appellations whose principal merit lies in being shorter and more phonetically harmonious than mere acronyms. But in and of themselves, Dexia, Vivendi, and Natexis are just about meaningless—except that they weren't chosen to please the external public but in order to resolve internal dilemmas such as dealing with touchy former or current stakeholders or displaying such and such a director's power and influence.

Even brands that have long maintained a relationship with the public fall into the error of bizarre justifications: the prize goes to Cacharel, which, at the launch of its men's perfume Nemo, outdid itself in the clarity and limpidity of its explanations: "In Nemo, there is an M, which is a center of universal magnetism. Just dive in, and then emerge from the word again. The same for Noa:[6] in all languages, N and O are linked to the state of mind. Moreover, Noa has three letters, while Nemo has four: $3 + 4 = 7$, yin and yang. In this way, the two perfumes can exist logically together." One wonders whether such considerations have the slightest chance of helping brand identity creation.

It takes a lot of time to become familiar with a name that has little meaning or that may have meaning, but not any visible link to what it designates: when Gap came to Europe, few were familiar with its history and its name (an allusion to the "generation gap," a phenomenon exaggerated by the hippy movement that everyone was talking about when the brand was created in California in 1969). Equally rare were those who had seen the brand make a 180 degree turn at the beginning of the 1980s and display black-and-white portraits that had a big impact on the history of American advertising. None of these original significations could be perceived, and Gap meant nothing except in English. Fortunately, massive investments dedicated to exporting the brand made it possible to associate the name immediately with a certain type of clothing and store, and in this way to latch on to a part of the brand's identity.

Lego has never meant anything (outside of Denmark, where the name is a contraction of "*Leg Godt*": "play well") but a building game using little colored plastic bricks. Only Richard Branson can tell us that Virgin was initially chosen to symbolize his ignorance of the rules in place in the business world. Who suspects that Melitta, the leading name in coffee filters, which sounds quite Italian, is in fact the first name of a German owner's grandmother? Who, outside of Germany and English-speaking countries, makes the connection between Nestlé ("nest" in English and German), the brand's symbol, and H. Nestlé's 1866 invention of "*farine lactée*" for babies? Who can say whether Swatch comes from the contraction of "Swiss watch" or "second watch"? Even at Swatch, nobody can remember, and today it no longer has the slightest importance.

In all cases, the meaning acquired in practice rapidly becomes more important than the initial meaning, when one existed, and the vicissitudes of practice diffract that initial meaning in an infinite number of ways: here as elsewhere, the most carefully laid plans often go awry. The name obviously is part of the brand's identity, but most of the time it's just a reference point whose implications are to be sought elsewhere than in the symbols that make it up.

The devil is in the details

Identity can come down to tiny things, details that we would be wrong to call minor: for example, the snaps on Petit-Bateau's cotton tops, a strong sign of identity, because the brand was the only one to equip its products with them.[7] Or else, a slight typographical change, but one that is deeply meaningful: lower-case instead of capital letters. Hewlett Packard and British Petroleum both chose this path to express their recent change of identity. HP and BP became "hp" and "bp," which was a way of abandoning a certain kind of superiority that had become "politically incorrect".

A schoolboy's slate above a bin of fruits and vegetables might appear purely decorative, but at Asda, in Great Britain, it was part of the new identity being constructed by the new leadership that took the reins of this popular supermarket chain in the 1990s. The new team of leaders considered the change in identity to be essential, and it took place through strategic decisions as well as the tweaking of details. Thus, in order to get back to the "roots of brand identity" by bringing prices down as far as possible, a drastic policy of cost reduction was put in place, and signified with the aid of details that might have seemed minor but that obviously weren't: thus, the mere fact of writing the price in chalk on a big slate above the fruit and vegetable aisle was a way of saying that every day, the person in charge of the aisle was seeking (and finding) the best possible prices in the region from local producers.[8]

Apple's move from a rainbow logo to one with no color at all, might also look like just a detail: after all, the apple was still the same. Steve Jobs, who was behind the choice of the rainbow and defended it tooth and nail despite the much higher costs it entailed, was also, it seems, responsible for phasing it out: he found it "dated". But Apple's entire identity was transformed: wasn't abandoning the colors often used in schools or children's bedrooms a way of saying: I've grown up? Wasn't giving up the symbol of the rainbow bridge between sky and earth a way of suggesting: now I have my feet on the ground, rather than my head in the clouds?

A detail as slender as a thread can help a brand to redefine an identity buffeted by turbulence, as shown by Levi's. "Levi's Engineered Jeans move with your body" wasn't just an ad campaign slogan but first and foremost the characteristic of an avatar of the famous 501 line, which had been undone and rebuilt by its consumers, and thus endowed with stretchy seams to better adapt to the wearer's movements, as well as lower back pockets, to make it easier to put hands in them, the whole thing made from a less rigid fabric than traditional denim.

Questions of design

Over time, the body of the brand produces such and such a sign that is more visible than the others: a logo here, a product there, or else a color, which ends up incarnating brand identity without anyone having wanted or chosen it to do so.

To ward off such random outcomes, some brands resort to an organization of forms that can concern all or a part of brand identity: product conception, conditioning, packaging, in-store advertising, etc. Some companies go so far as to shape the place where brand identity will be expressed, as we will see later on with the Spatial pole.

Designers are called upon to perform this kind of operation, and the best design firms have engaged in increasingly profound reflection about brand logic, going beyond the limits of "purely" visual identity: today, they're all selling "brand management," and have even made their lives easier—in the process causing much confusion in the business—by speaking bluntly of "branding."

What could be more logical? The shape, the color, and the material of an object are the first distinguishing elements that meet the eye, and they all bear meaning, but not in the way it's sometimes explained to readers hungry for simple, or even simplistic, formulas. Take, for example, the following mini-dictionary of colors and materials, taken from the French economic press:[9]

Red = passion
Blue = relaxation
White = cleanliness
Rock = solidity
Wood = warmth
Iron = manmade/technical nature

Nothing about this is completely false, but at the same time nothing is accurate either when it comes to associations of this sort. I've said it, and I'll say it again: meaning isn't in a color or a material *in itself*, but in their relationship with the rest of the elements that make up the brand or the product. A color doesn't exist on its own: it always has a shape and a material basis of some kind. And that shape and that material don't just float in the air, they exist within a grouping of objects, sounds, words, and people. It's this whole that has meaning, and not the shape of a door handle or the color of a carpet. In itself, a curved line has no more meaning than a straight one. But when it's applied to the design of a car headlight, and when that car is called a Jaguar, well, then it takes on meaning, the one specified by designer G. Lawson: "We've given eyes to our feline." Crossed seams on a handbag don't have much meaning in themselves, but if they form a quilted motif, we recognize Chanel, so much so that if we find the same motif on the frames of some eyeglasses whose logo is invisible, we'll assign them to the same brand.

Design obviously plays a key role in logo creation and redesign, whether the logo is just a name (YSL) or is accompanied by an image (Virgin's red star, the Lacoste crocodile) which sometimes takes on a life of its own and embodies the brand name on its own, as with the Michelin Man. Here the boundary between graphics and design is a blurry one. Which of the two words should be employed to evoke Lancôme's rose emblem? It's hard to say, but the fact is that the rose is so closely tied to Lancôme that it was reintroduced in its advertisements in 2008 after having been abandoned four years earlier. The logical consequences of this abandonment were that female consumers no longer saw any difference between Lancôme's advertisements and those of its competitors.

But in the best-case scenario, design creates brand identity in a much broader and more global way, and sometimes even comes before brand identity or serves as a replacement for it, if it is indeed true that a consumer's eye perceives color at thirty feet, shape at fifteen, and the brand at just three. On the shelf, the consumer can thus spot the little Actimel bottle, the Perrier bottle, the Absolut bottle, or the curved neck of Duck detergent containers well before they can read the brand name, and indeed this exposes them to the risk of being duped by an underhanded imitation.

Philips may be the brand that has gone the farthest in terms of using design to build its identity. "It's a question of authenticity," says the company. "A brand must reflect, in a transparent way, the values of the company behind it, just as an individual must act according to what we know about him. We seek to anticipate future needs, and our design reflects that already." Whence the association with Alessi for the manufacture of several products such as the Billy hand blender and the Vesta Pro webcam, which probably helped to redefine the brand's identity. And this attention to design concerns not only product development, but also packaging, display, and advertising: all points of contact with the consumer are concerned. "Since technology is the same for everyone, the form that it takes is what makes the difference," is the word from Philips Design,[10] which employs 450 people and works both for its mother company and for the business world at large.

Dyson owes everything to the design of the vacuum cleaner that made its designer, James Dyson, famous, and despite his reservations made him into the creator (he dislikes the word) of a world-renowned brand. Here, design should be understood as the marriage of aesthetics and function, in every sense of the term, from the narrowest (a pattern, a drawing) to the broadest, if we recall that a design is also an idea, a plan, a project. In this case, a plan hatched by an engineer who wasn't especially interested in the art of housecleaning, but who was using the vacuum at home one day and found that it lacked power. Seeking applications for "cyclonic" technology, and after thousands of trials, he managed to perfect the famous vacuum without a bag whose existence and high performance are known even to the Queen of England: it seems there are dozens of them at Buckingham Palace.

Without going so far as to radically revolutionize a market, without producing any major innovations, without even tweaking the product, packaging design can help bring out a brand's identity all on its own: this was the case with Absolut at the beginning, with the perfume CK be, and also with Grant's Whiskey, which looks to emerge from the pack by relying on the triangular shape of its bottles. Using little triangles also did a great deal to solidify The Laughing Cow's identity, and the same goes for Babybel's little red shells.

In general, when we think of design, we think of product design: cars, appliances, cosmetics, food. But design can also take part in creating brand identity as a whole. In this way, Scandinavian design, all by itself, has been instrumental for several brand identities, and rather well-known ones at that: Absolut, Ikea, Bang & Olufsen. After giving birth to boxy cars that seemed to have been carved out of a single block, Volvo is now clearly taking inspiration from the Swedish design tradition, and in particular from its timelessness and functionality, its concern for the client's well-being, and its attention to the slightest detail. "All of our work aims at creating spontaneous, even unconscious, recognition," says the head of design. The new watchwords: fluidity and dynamism, without neglecting either the safety angle or "a few of the brand's unique features: a large V shape sculpted on the hood, a generous radiator grill, a very pronounced lateral line joining the headlight to the taillights, the latter placed high on the back end."

Questions of price

It's obvious that price is part of brand identity: one of the first criteria for defining a brand is its pricing, and not only in cases where one is dealing with a high-end brand or, on the contrary, a very affordable one, but even between the two, in the middle range. Within the first minute of a nondirective interview, female consumers from the same socio-professional category will say, for example, of Banana Republic or Nine West, "it's expensive" or "it's affordable": for them price is an essential criterion, even when their opinions about the price fluctuate.

However, many of the brand identities that have recently emerged are at the extreme ends of the spectrum: either low-cost brands, like the budget airlines easyJet and Ryanair, or, on the contrary, high-end brands such as (in the air transport sector) the airlines offering transatlantic flights composed exclusively of "business class" seating. In the drinks category, by deliberately positioning itself at the high end ($10 more than Absolut), Grey Goose managed an unexpected breakthrough for a vodka that has nothing English, American, Scandinavian, or Russian about it—since it has been made for scarcely ten years in…Cognac, in France. The same goes for Swarovski, which for a king's ransom sells synthetic crystal (a glass high in lead) and extravagant jewels made from the same substance.

Sisley aspires to be "the most selective of the top twenty brands" of cosmetics on the French market. It has been able to gain notoriety thanks to a very expensive skincare cream, Sisleya, which generated a lot of press: the price is indubitably part of its identity, at the risk of eclipsing its other components (quality? performance?), and even though the competing brands have since caught up with and surpassed it in the race for the highest price.

In 1997, at Club Med, the drop in prices after the arrival of a new CEO (about – 30 %) changed the brand's identity even in the eyes of people who didn't go to the Club and thus couldn't verify for themselves whether it had changed or not. But the equation "low price = younger clientele" necessarily had an impact on the brand's identity, as well as on its image, territory, and positioning.

Ten years later, the inverse manoeuver: Club Med repositioned itself at the high end, and prices soared. Once again, those prices take part in forging the brand's identity.

However, on its own a price cannot create an enduring identity, much less a specific one, because even selective mass market brands are always overtaken by their competitors. Sisley was the first brand in France to sell skin creams for 200 euros; today, at least fifteen other brands do the same. Club Med keeps raising rates, but at the cost of such profound changes to its initial identity that this identity has been gradually blurred. Today, what advantages does it offer over similar companies that are just as expensive and just as luxurious?

THE SPATIAL POLE

A brand is a portion of space. In French, this is clear: according to the linguist Claude Hagège, the etymology of the word *marque* ("brand") comes from the Germanic *markjan*, a term that stems from a dialect whose traces can still be found today in the east of France, Belgium, and south-western Germany. *Markjan* means "a territory that is delimited and that confers identity". There is no use lingering over the usage to which marketing has put the notion of brand territory: it only confirms that however you approach the subject, whether from the Latin branch that culminates in the French "*marque*" (*marca* in Spanish, *marchio* in Italian), or from the Anglo-Saxon branch that leads to "brand," you end up with the same piece of land: either one where you farm, or one where you graze herds.

Brands *cannot* communicate outside of a material space. This space can be as small as a cell phone screen or as big as a theme park, as is the case with Disneyland. It can be spread out over ten-story posters, like Nike, or reduced to the size of a soda machine on a train station platform, like

Evian. It can have the square footage of a baggage carrousel in an airport (Virgin Atlantic) or of a crosswalk (a Mr. Clean campaign).[11] But whether it's big or small, visible or invisible, real or imaginary, space is an unavoidable aspect of all communication, and brand communication (which, let us recall, includes the totality of signals given off by the brand even in the absence of any advertising) is no exception.

For brands, there are several ways of working with this spatial dimension:

- either it refers to a real or imaginary "elsewhere";

- or else it locates itself "here" and appropriates a specific space;

- or else it looks for a way out of this dichotomy.

Let it be noted that one brand's "elsewhere" is another brand's "here," which raises difficulties and necessitates adjustments when brands develop internationally.

Elsewhere

One of the chief functions of brands, as we know, is to guarantee provenance, to make it so that faced with such and such an object that you haven't seen manufactured, all uncertainty about its quality is banished by the guarantee of its birthplace. Indeed, in Europe, long before there were brands in the legal sense that we give the term today, the best products often claimed a specific origin: Lyon silk, eau de Cologne, Czech or Venetian glassware, Bruges lace, and so on.

Brand identities do the same thing today, even if the system has become considerably more sophisticated, and the space fragmented in pieces that can be big or small, sharply or hazily defined.

The food industry is perhaps the sector—but not the only one—where the affirmation of origins is still at the basis of a large number of brand identities, some of which are practically like a label. Of course, geographical anchoring (at the regional or national level) is all the stronger when the country or region in question is itself a kind of brand: Parmigiano Reggiano belongs to Northern Italy, Evian to the French alps, Cardhu whiskey to the Speyside region in Scotland. The same is true for metropolises like New York (DKNY, Maybelline New York) or Paris, which acts as a powerful symbolic setting for numerous French luxury brands, notably Yves Saint-Laurent, with perfumes like Paris, Parisienne, and Rive Gauche, which is also a ready-to-wear clothing line. Even a city like Detroit can occasionally serve to reinforce brand identity, as was recently illustrated by the "Chrysler, imported from Detroit" campaign.

The same goes for the national level; some countries are brands in themselves, and use this fact with more or less skill for tourist attraction purposes. Morocco is a brand, as are Greece, Japan, and India (see the "Incredible India" campaign). But Porto Cruz has also done a great deal to sing the praises of a "country where black is colorful," as has Martini for Italy, whose boot periodically appears in its advertisements. St. Ives cosmetics always specifies "Swiss formula," and the hair-care products brand Aussie is immediately recognized as Australian (non-English speakers can come to the same conclusion by observing the little kangaroo that accompanies the logo and that leaps along the neck of the bottles). Old Virginia bears its name like a southern flag, and, so that there will be no mistake, it adds, "Roots of Bourbon". With a very basic product (simple plastic flip-flops), Havaianas has managed to give itself not a Hawaiian brand identity, as one might have thought (that's the meaning of the word in Portuguese), but a Brazilian one, and is very proud of this.[12] As for Ikea, its Swedish origins are visible everywhere: in the logo's colors, in the design and the product names, in its food court, and even in the company's philosophy.

Bacardi deliberately used the spatial pole to present itself as a Puerto Rican (and not Cuban) rum by sponsoring the Bacardi Folk Arts Fair. This could be interpreted as a classic case of marketing manipulation, which is what it is, except that the means employed are beyond all suspicion of artifice. Bacardi worked with an official government agency responsible with deciding what Puerto Rican-ness is (or isn't). It accepted only artists who were registered with that government agency, and soon the festival acquired a good reputation for being "authentic" rather than commercial.[13]

Guinness cultivates its Irish origins and character. San Pellegrino periodically goes back to its origins and invites consumers to "live in Italian". Burberry recently made a spectacular come-back by reinventing itself without denying its British origins, a savvy mixture of "conformism and extravagance, romanticism and humor." And, to remain in Albion, think of the images that accompany this advertisement: "You are entering the land of the Clan Campbell", or the following declaration: "Talisker is the only single malt Scotch whiskey made by the sea on the shores of the Isle of Skye."

However, it is possible to make a mistake about a country's identity, and when a brand identity is based on this error, its foundation is weakened. That's what happened a few years ago to Bally, whose redeployment strategy was based (among other elements) on "Switzerland, the brand's country of origin, a country with a rich history in graphic arts, architecture, and design". Nobody questioned the truth of this statement, it was simply that public perception didn't match it: for most people, Switzerland means mountains, William Tell, and chocolate. Mountains of clichés, it is true—and I could cite others—but either one has the budget, time, and means necessary to change collective mentalities, or one has to make do with them. When, in addition, a character trait rightly or wrongly attributed to national identity (where Switzerland is concerned, for example, I am thinking of slowness), is at the heart of the brand's image and its problems (Bally had fallen into a deep slumber), the two phenomena are mutually reinforcing.

Before it wagered everything on the Swiss tradition of industrial design, Bally would have had to work for several years in the Swiss tourism office until mountain pastures, white wine from the Valais region, and Toblerone gave way to Le Corbusier in the public's imagination.

There is no need to lay claim to an entire country to activate the Spatial pole: a few square meters can be enough. Hewlett Packard, which for a long time, purely on principle, was hostile to advertising, decided only belatedly to speak out as a brand (rather than simply displaying its products). It did so by evoking its mythical birthplace, the famous garage at 367, Addison Avenue in Palo Alto, which gave birth to the no-less-famous "HP Way". It figures in one of the ads in the first major press campaign of 1999, accompanied by the words "Rules of the Garage."

But the difficulty with the Spatial pole is that "elsewhere" and "here" are always relative terms. Brazil, Guatemala, Columbia, or Kenya can be used by Jacques Vabre to give French people a sense of exoticism that reinforces the brand's quest for identity (vouching for the provenance of the various coffees). But this campaign can hardly be used to sell Jacques Vabre in any of those countries. Aside from American brands, which are always ready to declare "We are the world", most major national brands rarely sell to locals by singing the praises of their own country. In France, Evian embroiders on the theme of eternal youth rather than on that of a spring water from the Alps.

If they do speak of their own country, brands do so by emphasizing a particular region, like L'Occitane. And whether this elsewhere is real (as for L'Occitane en Provence) or imaginary (the North Face), it nonetheless does a favor to the brands that make use of it. Obao, which now belongs to Garnier, itself part of the L'Oréal group, has never been a Japanese brand, but from the beginning it has constructed its identity on the image that Westerners have of Japan, even if this leads to absurd mistakes such as a "bubble bath" unheard of in Japanese ritual. Little matter, *re*-representations are what we're dealing with here, and there is ample room for each country to introduce interpretations, faithful or otherwise, of an elsewhere tailored for a custom fit.

Yet as soon as a brand acquires an international reputation, it becomes necessary to switch the "here" and "elsewhere" categories incessantly. With roots in New York, as its name suggests, DKNY has become an American brand, but in Europe and Asia, where it is distributed, it still has something essentially New York about it, which is impossible to confuse with a Texan or Californian brand, for example. In the Big Apple, it's at home, and it can thus say "here"; as soon as it leaves, it comes from elsewhere. Nicolas Feuillatte champagne has capitalized on this phenomenon by declaring in its campaigns that it is from "Epernay—New York—Beyond".

Here

In general, it's distribution that is best able to manipulate the spatial context, whether it's a matter of setting up brands under a global banner, or opening a store under the banner of such and such a brand, something that is increasingly frequent. The place where a brand is found says a lot about it: remaining in the pharmacy circuit, as Vichy does in Europe, or leaving it, like Biotherm, both in the L'Oréal Group, inevitably has an influence on public perception.

Even without changing location, space is eloquent: everywhere the brand took root the day it left the confines of Spain, Zara immediately gave itself the stature of a major brand by opening big shops on prestigious thoroughfares, even though most women had never heard of it.

But it is also possible to abandon the idea of acquiring 5,000 square feet on the Champs-Elysées so as to remain, for example, at an "historic" address, and manipulate the space that one possesses in such a way as to change the brand's discourse: this is what interior renovations and merchandizing are for. In this way, Agnès B., without doing anything very revolutionary, made a subtle but decisive change by renovating the changing rooms, which went from being collective to individual. Just a detail? Not completely. In this case, the brand's identity owes everything to its creator, who has never made any effort to hide her political opinions. Going from a shared to a private space was a way for her to say farewell to the "Left Bank-ism" of her early years.

But the solution most often employed these days delights real estate agents—it consists in opening retail spaces in the name of the brand (sometimes baptized "*espaces*", as was the case with Pierre Cardin in the 1970s), even if this means confusing matters to such an extent that a new hybrid emerges, somewhere between a brand and a retail space. In the end, this is a distinction that only specialists make. As for consumers, they simply speak of brands, whether they're talking about Carrefour, H&M, or Diesel.

Examples abound, even if one doesn't take into account what consumers call "chains," especially where ready-to-wear clothing is concerned, which are pure and simple sales points, cookie-cutter stores that are pretty much identical because they are all based on the same concept. As soon as a retail space becomes a living space, this implies that space has indeed become a major aspect of brand identity. We've seen this happening of late with experiential marketing,[14] which is more and more popular today. Here, it is not a matter of design, merchandizing, or interior decoration—or at least not only.

That Nivea should open a three-story Nivea Haus right in the middle of Hamburg, with a hair salon, a massage parlor, a beauty parlor, and a "well-being space," all at reasonable prices, is unusual but, all things considered, logical--unlike experiments such as the one imagined by LG with its "wash bar," a cross between two usually separate spaces, the café and the laundromat. On the other end of the price scale, Baccarat left its musty old Parisian headquarters and, with much pomp and circumstance, and in a fashionable part of town, opened a sumptuous "Maison Baccarat," at once showroom, museum, art gallery, and restaurant. The first "spaces" opened by Nespresso in Paris were along similar lines, with little boutiques where one could sit down and read the newspaper or read a book from the in-house library while sipping a coffee on the house, and without even being obliged to buy anything on the way out.

Megastores are also in vogue, beginning with Niketown or Hershey's Chocolate World, and followed by various "spaces" (Paul Ricard,[15] in Paris), and Foundations, like the Cartier Foundation, which "is an integral part of the brand" and strongly works for its identity. Even bigger than megastores, of course, there are entertainment parks, as famous as Disneyland or Disneyworld, or as new as the Ferrari World Abu Dhabi, to this day "the world's larger indoor theme park".

But it's not enough to open a shop, a stadium, a building, a theater, a museum, or a park using the brand's name. If brand identity isn't transposed with the greatest care, it's bound to draw criticism, as was the case with the Jaguar boutique. The press may hasten to point out, for example, that "aficionados are unlikely to recognize the plush, sporty lines of their 'E' type," and that "the bright light, the burr elm of the side paneling, a bit too shiny and proliferating everywhere, and the radiator caps reproduced in all sizes, including on a pair of shoes (and in gold no less!)" are at the very least in extremely dubious taste. In such cases, the backlash is never long in coming.

Nowhere/everywhere

There are brands that try to escape the law of place. Of course, they never succeed except with smoke and mirrors, but their attempts are nonetheless interesting to observe.

This is the case with luxury brands, or with ready-to-wear clothing brands. Thus, not long ago Cartier declared : "All over the world, in the name of a single, unique identity, we are setting up the same advertisements, the same kind of events, and the same catalogues and window displays, which will change in all countries at the same time." Gucci, Vuitton, Dior, and Ralph Lauren could easily say just about the same thing.

The same holds for Gap (and naturally for the same reasons, having to do with economies of scale): "Once they're in one of our stores, the client shouldn't know whether they're in New York, Paris, or Tokyo." A similar impression can be felt with numerous other brands or brand labels, as becomes clear when traveling: whether you are in an English city, a Texas airport, or an Indonesian shopping center, you find the same stores everywhere, the same décors, the same products, with just a few slight variations: The Body Shop, Ikea, Sephora, Benetton, and Zara almost make you lose your sense of direction because the identity of these brands is identical from place to place and country to country.

And contrary to what is thought, it's not giants like Coca-Cola and McDonald's that impose their identity with the greatest force, but rather the fashion and cosmetics sectors, from the top to the bottom of the price range, once a certain level of power has been achieved.

McDonald's, for example, which we think of as a tank crushing everything in its path without worrying about hurting anyone's feelings, is on the contrary always modulating its identity, and doing so in a way that is much deeper than Gap or Vuitton: the capital M is not always yellow (it can be metallic grey when local ordinances require it), is not always stuck on the top of a pole, the décor is not always in shocking colors and pure plastic, and the menu changes with the country. McDonald's may be "everywhere" but certainly not "nowhere": nothing is dearer to its ear than being at once "here" and "elsewhere," American *and* Australian in Australia, Chinese in China, Turkish in Turkey, Indian in India, and so on.

In a different way, Starbucks has adroitly manipulated the Spatial pole not in the way McDonald's has, but rather by creating an "intermediate place" where the consumer likes to take a break between home and office. Nothing so new in that, people from the Latin countries will say, since they invented the bistro and are in the habit of spending a lot of time on café terraces. And besides, the founder of Starbucks, H. Schultz, doesn't hide the fact that he brought back his idea (good coffee + a place to

drink it in peace) from a trip to Italy. But in the United States, the introduction of this "intermediate place" was meaningful and had no trouble
catching on.

Timberland repositioned itself based on a universal "elsewhere" by adopting "Adventure Anywhere" as its new signature. Aigle is trying to do the
same thing: "Aigle, For the reintroduction of man into nature," which leads
the brand into distant, but unidentified, lands, that is to say everywhere in
the world. For its part, TBS declares "Welcome to Planet Ocean," an astute
way of taking the brand around the globe, but nowhere in particular.

With "Terre d'Hermès," a men's perfume, Hermès has created a space of
its own, one that exists nowhere but in its brand symbolism, an advertising
universe composed of vast spaces that cannot be placed on a map.

And yet the best way of being at once everywhere and nowhere is to
be a nomad, on the move, always traveling. The annals of advertising history have recorded the long period (twenty years) during which Vuitton has
occupied this shifting territory with its "Spirit of Travel" tagline, affixed
under magnificent landscape photos by Jean Larivière. The same theme has
made a resurgence over the last few years, but with a significant inversion:
travel has given way to travelers, and to immobile travelers sitting in a car
(Gorbachev), on a train station platform (Catherine Deneuve), a tree branch
next to a beach (Sean Connery), or in a dinghy (Angelina Jolie).

This halt in the voyage, this move toward personal (and here highly per-
sonalized) space probably corresponds to a profound trend in Western societies, for it is also found at the antipodes of the luxury universe, in a brand
born on the Internet in January 2003. It bears the name of a social network
that is especially popular with musicians, and if we needed proof that the
Web hasn't changed the rules of the game for constructing identity, we have
it here in the new brand's recourse to space as a pivot point. The brand's
name? MySpace.

THE TEMPORAL POLE

Brands can only exist over time. The biggest ad campaign in the world
wouldn't be able to grant brand status overnight to an unknown name.
It only took five years for Amazon.com to acquire the status of a major
brand—but it still took five years. With apologies to CEOs impatient for
overnight conquests and striving to repair in a few weeks the damage
caused by years of negligence, time—extended time—is an unavoidable
given in the life of brands.

The same goes for Internet brands. Some of them already seem to us to be
anchored very solidly in place, like Google, eBay, Facebook, and Yahoo!,

but this is to forget that we are at the very beginnings of their journey. In France alone at the beginning of the twentieth century there were more than 400 car brands, most of which felt justified in looking ahead to a promising future. Today, three remain, two of which belong to the same company. It's very likely that the same thing will happen to internet brands, the only difference being that things will get sorted out a bit more quickly.

Another reason why time is an unavoidable given for brands already came up earlier: we only know what we recognize, what we've seen before, what we've perceived or understood in the recent or distant past. In other words, what we don't recognize has no meaning. Nicolas Hayek, the founder and CEO of Swatch, expresses this clearly: "That which is neither visible nor recognizable bears no message."

There are many ways to manipulate the temporal pole. The simplest way of getting our bearings is to note:

- how a brand plays with the past;

- how it appeals to the future;

- how it treats the present.

These three categories are not mutually exclusive: some brands manage to activate all three at the same time.

Manipulating the past

There is no identity without memory: this truth, which is recognized by all who work on memory phenomena, is equally true of brands. Awareness is nothing other than the measure of that memory, and it's a possession that is so precious that it plays a considerable role in brand capital evaluations performed by financial auditing firms.

In fact, in the eyes of some specialists, memory comes before the construction of identity, which is why most analyses of identity begin with an exploration of the brand's past. That past is both the company's past and the consumer's past: at once the sum of individual memories, and a collective memory. The way in which these two memories work and interact is a complex subject that merits a book-length study of its own: how does the contagion of ideas[16] and representations take place? How are memories reworked? Why distinguish between strong and weak memory or between long- and short-term memory? What is truly memorable? These are just a few of the questions that must be asked before going ahead with the indispensable revision of methods for measuring memorization, a revision that advertisers, agencies, and research firms should collectively undertake if they truly want to make brand communication more effective.

In fact, even when one is put in charge of a brand with the firm intention of making it evolve, it's impossible to erase the past, whether that past is illustrious, questionable, or both at once. Whether one likes it or not, brand identity must be dealt with, and one of the sources of identity is the brand's history.

Generally speaking, it is thought that this history is a treasure and an attribute that one should be proud of. Brands that have such a history miss no opportunity to celebrate it (except at Fiat, where the brand's centennial, in 1999, gave rise to no special celebrations "for fear of seeming too old") and a thirtieth, fiftieth, or (with even greater fanfare) one-hundredth anniversary is always a very good reason to activate the Temporal pole. Michelin, Nivea, Hershey's or Bacardi, among many others, thus publicly blew out the numerous candles on their respective birthday cakes, and are all the better off for having done so.

The same benefit accrued to Van Cleef & Arpels: one hundred years and three new collections to celebrate the event (but on the theme of nature, to signify continuity).

The famous water babies synchronized swimming spot launched by Evian in 1998 was also a way for the brand to recall its past as a brand that used to be presented as "baby's water". Water for baby bottles, of course, which fifty years later became water (for the same babies, just a little older) "approved by your body as a source of youth".

Another way of using the Temporal pole is to go back to the brand's origins, which can be done explicitly—1664 beer has its birth date as its name—or implicitly. In 1986, Cadbury thus went back to its original trade of chocolate maker, after a lackluster period of diversification due to its merger with Schweppes. Lacoste periodically highlights its legendary polo shirt, for example, in order to counter the perverse effects of the brand's hijacking by clientele categories that risked making the brand commonplace or even diminishing its value. And going back to roots can take place within the exclusive history of the brand itself, as when watch-maker Breguet recalls that it invented the Tourbillon mechanism, or else it can recall a common past, one that is known and loved, such as Laura Ashley's Victorian England.

The problem is that "getting back to one's roots" can sometimes cause a narrowing of focus that in the long run hurts the brand more than it helps. Levi's, on the decline in the early 1980s, managed to emerge from the crisis with the famous "back to our roots" maneuver, thanks to a strong advertising policy highlighting its 501 line, which became the reference point for the jeans market. Fifteen years later, a new crisis: since the baby boomer generation swore by their 501 jeans, their children, quite naturally, refused to buy them. By centering the brand on a single point of identity (the 501 line accounts for half of worldwide sales), Levi's deprived itself of other forms of expression. Should 501 falter, the whole brand stumbles with it.

The weight of memory is so strong and plays such an integral role in memory that some brands don't hesitate to invent the past they never had: Tod's with its movie stars from before the invention of Tod's. Absolut isn't really wrong to put "since 1879" on its bottles, but it's still a bit of slight-of-hand: the date is really that of the high-temperature distillation method imported from France by L. Ollson Smith, the Swedish merchant whom Absolut made its adoptive father when they decided to give themselves a fictional past. In the same way, Abbaye de Leffe Belgian beer plays with dates by pretending to have been born in 1240. This isn't false (1240 is the date the brewery was founded, the abbey having been built in the preceding century), but to hew strictly to the truth, Leffe would have to add the long series of dates corresponding to the deaths and resurrections that have marked its history: the floods of 1466, the devastation wrought by Charles the Bold's invasion of Flanders, more devastation during the French Revolution, and then World War II, which ravaged Northern Europe in the twentieth century. And it shouldn't be forgotten that there is no relationship whatsoever between the beer brewed at the Leffe abbey in the Middle Ages for the needs of monks and pilgrims and the beer currently manufactured under the same name by the world's biggest beer producer (in volume), Interbrew.

Keeping traditions alive is another way to bring back the past: that was Jaguar's strategy when it employed 150 cabinetmakers to cut, install, and polish the side panels in burr walnut that are an intrinsic part of the brand's identity, as are the round shapes that Jaguar has come back to after giving more angular ones a try. Fidelity to tradition was also behind the "Open House" operation organized by Vuitton in October, 2011, during which the public was invited to visit some of the brand's studios.

The past can also be extended or revived by reactivating it through allusion, which can be accomplished with delicate little touches, as when Dior jewelers put several of its "Gourmette" rings on miniature gray and white Louis XVI chairs against a background of carpet and molding, to suggest the classical décor of the era when the brand was called Christian Dior. But it's also possible to go about this in a way that's much less localized and more global, as Volkswagen did when launching the New Beetle, which followed in the footsteps of the legendary Beetle. A flower power, hippy car, and such a cult brand that it became a movie star (recall *The Love Bug* and *Harold and Maud*), the Beetle had been the best-selling car in the world in the days before the New Beetle came along. Thirty years later, how was the New Beetle presented? "Less flower, more power," was the slogan, with the cars arranged like petals in a flower pattern. This was a way of reviving memories associated with the brand while at the same time remaining in a present moment where the driver is now more important than his or her car. And to underscore both the leap ahead and the ties with the past, the New Beetle even went so far as to present itself by saying, "If you sold your soul in the 80s, here's your chance to buy it back."

The above example shows that change and continuity can go together, and that lasting just to last is not a worthy goal in itself, and doesn't necessarily generate positive effects on brand identity. On the headstones of the brand cemetery, there are hundreds of brands with old birthdates that did nothing to prevent them from fading away. For every Abbaye de Leffe, how many breweries have sunk into oblivion, how many cheese, wine, and clothing brands have disappeared or been forgotten? Lalique and Daum, to cite but two French crystal brands, may have a prestigious past, but who's to say whether this will be enough to keep them alive?

Manipulating the present

It happens that without beating around the bush a brand declares that it belongs to the present, as the jeweler O.J. Perrin once did by deeming itself "resolutely contemporary," no doubt in order to stand out from its peers, all of whom, or at least most, were very concerned to appear old and venerable. Hermès recently took the same tack, calling itself a "contemporary artisan since 1837."

But most of the time, the present is activated in a way that is less direct, although perfectly clear.

The first way of playing on the present is to surf on the waves of current (or recurrent) events, as Mr. Clean did by building around exceptional or recurring events throughout the year (Mother's Day, the Olympic Games, Halloween, etc.).

Sometimes the surfing takes place on longer waves, deep trends, and current social issues and general concerns are integrated into the brand's identity. Launching products specifically aimed at countering the effects of the sun's rays, even beyond summer vacation, is a way for brands to latch on to current events and trends, as Clinique did with its Cityblock cream or Clarins with UV Plus. The same rationale applies to Ariel, which has taken alerts about global warming and its impact on the environment into account by launching a campaign encouraging people to change their cleaning habits, a campaign that could easily be a collective campaign for detergents in general since instead of vaunting the merits of Ariel, the brand advises against prewashing laundry in the washing machine, and recommends washing at less than 90 degrees Fahrenheit.

The Laughing Cow has transformed this little game of leapfrog into an art form: first advertised as a very filling, fatty cheese (which was an advantage right after World War II in Europe), it has regularly changed its tune over the years, finally becoming, in its low-fat version, the guest star of a fashionable weight-loss program, the South Beach Diet, while in Britain it presents itself as a good source of…Omega 3s, so as not to let any opportunity for seeming healthy pass it by.

Another way of becoming part of the present consists in playing with the brand's periodicity, in the press sector, for example, where one is necessarily categorized either as a "daily" (*Daily Mirror, USA Today*), a "weekly" (*Newsweek*), or a monthly (*The Atlantic Monthly*). When *Le Monde*, a daily newspaper, added a monthly periodical, *Le Monde 2*, it was indeed a matter of its "relationship to time". The editorial director, E. Plenel, explained at the time:

> *Le Monde*'s new formula, launched in 1995, mixes temporalities. Besides up-to-the-minute information, we are interested in presenting a series of investigative reports or point-of-view pieces that unfold at a weekly or even a monthly rhythm. But a daily is ephemeral. There are thus a lot of texts that vanish through the sieve of time. The idea of *Le Monde 2* is to offer an overview of the past month, one that can serve as a reference for the future.

Still in the press sector, it's also possible to play on the time it takes to read or watch the magazine or program (*20 Minutes*), the moment it appears on newsstands (*The London Evening Standard, Il Corriere della sera*), the rapidity with which it disseminates information (*L'Express*) or the way the publication coincides perfectly with its era (*Time Magazine, The New York Times*, or *The Times* in the UK).

But the periodicity game isn't played just by the press—"limited series" make it possible to play the game in just about any sector. The basis of Swatch's policy is, among other things, the rapid rotation of collections in a trade where such things didn't exist before. Following the example of Estee Lauder, cosmetics brands have also acquired the habit of putting out makeup "collections" twice a year, just like fashion brands. Chanel, Dior, Gucci, and Hermès all make "time-sensitive" products, a phenomenon that isn't unique to luxury brands or reserved exclusively for perfumes and cosmetics, as is shown by the success of seasonal alliances between mass-distributed brands like H&M and a designer who may be from the haute couture world (Karl Lagerfeld) or from a more democratic tradition (Marimekko, the legendary Finnish brand).

Some brands take an even more active role in the temporal pole, for example by launching a product that helps the consumer save time, as Lavazza did in Italy in the 1950s by selling the first ground coffee. Or when Uncle Ben's came up with a pre-cooking process for rice (which had already been brought down to ten minutes instead of the twenty or twenty-five minutes required for traditional cooking), which enabled it to display the cooking time in large lettering on the package: "Two minutes, express cooking." Or when Fairy Platinum Detergent promised to act in ten minutes, whereas it used to take a whole night to clean a load of very dirty dishes.

FedEx revolutionized the transport of merchandise with its "overnight delivery" principle, working on the Temporal pole in two of its dimensions: brevity and punctuality. McDonald's set up the Made For You system, which was supposed to reduce the wait time at the register. When it arrived in France, Amazon.fr launched a 24-hour delivery service, obliging its local competitors to do the same. For several years, many e-commerce sites have also been offering delivery in 24 or 48 hours thanks to agreements with vendors located near big city centers. Grand Optical changed the landscape of the eyewear market by becoming "the optician that makes glasses in an hour or less."

The battle to gain time is now a universal one, and the internet is obviously a valuable tool for winning that battle, not only thanks to websites, which offer a means of interfacing directly with consumers, but also at an earlier stage. For example, certain insurance companies have set up long-distance appraisal programs: the mechanic films the damaged car with a digital video camera and sends the tape to the appraiser who, without leaving the office, can evaluate the cost of the parts and labor and send back an estimate. The system works for nearly 50 % of material damages and makes it possible to save considerable time.

But it also happens that a brand manipulates time not to speed it up but rather to slow it down, and in doing so reinforces its identity. Guinness bets on the fact that while people are in a hurry today, there are still some things they're willing to wait for—a Guinness stout, for example. The beer has to be drawn from the tap and then allowed to settle. This waiting period is part of the enjoyable experience of drinking a Guinness.[17]

Another way of stretching time: instead of making products that are built to wear out, offer a product of such good quality that it lasts much longer than the competitor's products. Better yet, when the product starts to wear out, offer to repair it instead of throwing it away and replacing it with a new one. That's the strategy at Mephisto, a brand known for the quality, comfort, and durability of its shoes, which can be brought in for repairs even fifteen years after purchase.

There's yet a third solution, which consists neither in shrinking nor in stretching time but in compressing it: the French national rail service SNCF decided to develop the TGV brand when it discovered that the new train was able to embody both quantitative and qualitative time: the passenger goes faster, and the trip becomes time for enjoying life rather than a form of constraint, because you're free to read, play cards, rent a DVD, or do the crossword, work, or do nothing. Which makes it possible to say: "TGV, take the time to go fast."

Finally, there's the solution that consists in creating one's own time, and attaching one's brand to it. That's what Swatch very logically did, by inventing a new temporal unit, Swatch Internet Time, which does away with time zones and makes it possible for denizens of the web to make appointments without risk of confusing the time in Tokyo with the time in Johannesburg or Rio de Janeiro.

Conversely, the phrase "A Hermès watch has all the time in the world" appears regularly above some of the brand's models.

But it's true that in its way, Hermès has also created its own time, a doubly rapid time in some sense: one for the so-called "timeless" products, which are designed by in-house teams, and another for products destined to live no more than two or three years, which are entrusted to external designers. Outside Hermès, time passes, more slowly than it does elsewhere, perhaps, but it passes, while within Hermès, it is suspended.

Manipulating the future

It is by definition infinitely more difficult to manipulate the future than the past: it's possible to make the past say a great many things. It's possible to do the same for the future, except that there's always the risk of being forgotten, proven wrong, or ignored by consumers, who are more interested in what's being offered to them here and now than in what will be happening (or failing to happen) in twenty years.

This is why few brands evoke the future, except in a vague manner and without making any hard and fast commitments. Sometimes it's merely on the occasion of an ad campaign, like the one for the new Jeep Grand Cherokee, which predicted: "One day I'll find Atlantis" or else "One day you'll find the Cities of Gold." But by definition this campaign remains localized, it doesn't insert the brand in a long-term future and concerns only the product (in this case the Grand Cherokee, not Jeep). There must be a tagline intended to last at least two or three years if the desire to be tied to the future is to have any truly profound effects on brand identity.

Sometimes, brands also make clearer and thus riskier predictions about the future, such as those made by Rado watches ("Shaping the future"). And finally, there are radical pronouncements: Patek Philippe declares, "We've never made a quartz watch, and we never will." And Jack Daniel's, thumbing its nose at the classic "Never say never": "We're not about to change. Not now, not ever."

Aiming for eternity

It took a series crises weathered by the Atlanta-based firm in 1999, in Europe and elsewhere in the world, for Coca-Cola to stop proclaiming "Always Coca-Cola." The adoption of a new slogan ("Enjoy"), announced with great fanfare, didn't stop the professional press from noting that beneath the guise of a great transformation in its advertising, Coca-Cola hadn't really changed much and continued to roll out the same old advertising locomotive pulling the same old railway cars filled with delirious adolescents accompanied by a "youthful" musical backdrop. Except that the change in slogan included two significant details: the name of the brand no longer appeared in the tagline, and, above all, Coca-Cola gave up trying to couple itself with "Always". This was a true revolution for a megabrand whose directors have been known to say, "We have two main principles: we're everywhere, and we'll always be there."[18]

At least they're frank: many brands are after the same goal, but they don't come right out and say so. It's true that aiming for eternity is a bit like believing one is God, which is an ambition that few sock or electric coffee-maker brands would confess to harboring. But other sectors have no such scruples. A champagne brand will say, without beating around the bush: "The Tattinger moment—make it last an eternity." And to ensure that we get the message, the champagne bottle is plunged into an ice bucket filled with…diamonds (which, as everyone knows, have been eternal ever since the famous De Beers campaign).

Generally speaking, brands from the luxury world have a tendency to think they're more immortal than the rest. They signify this in various ways. Some go so far as to proclaim their intention of "turning their back on time" (Jaeger le Coultre), or they name a perfume "Eternity" (Calvin Klein), or claim to offer "The Gift of Time" (Hermès, 2012). Most watch brands invoke the past: among others, Tag Heuer ("Swiss avant-garde since

1860"), Breguet ("since 1775"), and Blancpain ("A tradition of innovation since 1735"). But one of their preferred methods consists in presenting themselves clad in only their name and their date of birth. Thus Boucheron fills the whole space of a newspaper ad with a watch surrounded by a delicate halo against a deep blue background (perhaps to suggest that it's a divine object?), and accompanied simply by the phrase "Jeweler since 1872". As if time had begun unfolding at that moment and was destined to keep doing so without end.

Same thing with the famous perfume "L'Air du Temps" by Nina Ricci, which became a brand in its own right, even more powerful than the mother-brand, and whose successive reincarnations create a kind of cycle (the cycle of time is, as we know, that of eternal return). Another perfume by Guerlain, "L'Instant", seemed, by dint of its name alone, destined for a similar future, since in theory it could be reinterpreted again and again with the passing years.

Some ready-to-wear brands have also attempted to drop out of the time race and to chase not so much fashion as a new style. This is a paradox typical of Armani's approach, which makes it possible to recognize the cut of its clothes independently of the year in which they were produced.

In any event, one has to choose: one can try to be a "timeless brand" while seeking to "follow the trends," but only at the risk of confusing a clientele that has difficulty understanding how the same brand—Bally—can sell Louis XV walking shoes to grandmothers and tennis shoes à la Prada to their granddaughters.

And yet it seems easier to be eternal by keeping up with the present than by trying to escape it. Sartre said that nobody can become immortal without belonging resolutely to their own era. Some brands think the same way. In 1995, the president of Chaumet declared:

> Luxury brands were able to exist because they came up with great ideas from the beginning. They didn't go looking for ideas in past centuries, but in their own time. Thus Chaumet, which is the oldest jeweler,[19] has always belonged to its era: romantic in the 19th century, Art nouveau in the early 20th, and then Art deco. Today, luxury brands have trouble taking their noses out of the archives. In fifty years, I will have left no trace at Chaumet unless it can be said that during the 1990s the brand bore witness to its age.

One hears the same tune at Lancôme: "A luxury brand is a brand that knows how to renew itself and to change with the times" and also at Hermès, which changes themes every year in order to renew the brand's message and remain in sync with its era without falling into the bottomless pit of fashion. It is in this sense that it can claim to be a "contemporary artisan since 1837", just like Tag Heuer, "Swiss avant-garde since 1860".

THE NORMS POLE

The issue of continuity and change is so fundamental and so recurrent for brands that the answer, or at least the source, for many of the questions they ask themselves can be found in the Norms pole. This pole is based on the idea that no communication process (and let us recall that I'm looking at brands as one big process of communication) can take place outside of a social space structured by norms. Preexisting norms. There is no such thing as virgin territory where communication is concerned.

With respect to these norms, a brand can adopt four positions:

- uphold;

- respect;

- modulate;

- transgress.

In practice, these four positions can be boiled down to two:

- respect the norm;

- ignore or violate the norm in order to create a new one, an approach that some brands suggest with their name alone (Gap, for example, which creates a chasm between itself and its predecessors).

We just have to figure out what norms we're talking about. Here I'll exclude legal norms that brands are obliged to obey. Since a brand is fundamentally a difference, it is when it is free to follow or not to follow a rule that it has the chance to establish its identity. It's thus a matter of taking into account norms that are unwritten but known and globally followed by everyone, such as:

- the advertising norm (Don't show sad or ugly people);

- the industry norm (A moped has two wheels, not three);

- the product norm (Computers are for professional use only);

- the brand norm (We never did that before);

- the social and/or cultural norm (Don't eat with your fingers).

The advertising norm

This is the most visible but not necessarily the most crucial norm. It's also the one that's easiest to transgress, up to a certain point: all one has to do is to go against the grain of current practices and habits in a given sector or country.

Tag Heuer, a brand born in 1985 of the buyout of Heuer by Tag, managed in just a few years to make excellent breakthroughs in visibility and image by adopting a resolutely new and aggressive tone in a usually very subdued and classic, not to say dull, sector—advertising campaigns for watch brands, which were generally limited to a close-up photo of the product.

With striking black-and-white sports images (and for once, without featuring sailing, the favorite sport of numerous luxury brands), the prevailing advertising norm in the sector was happily revolutionized. Since, the brand has returned to the rank and file, like many of its competitors, by choosing another norm: using celebrity spokespersons.

Lavazza has tried to stand out in a very crowded sector by breaking the advertising mold thanks to a determinedly original campaign, one that plays on the Italian reputation for unbridled fantasy and strong artistic sensibility.

Mauboussin, for its part, has rebuilt its identity by deliberately ignoring the advertising standards in the high-end jewelry sector, an exclusive club of which the brand has nonetheless been a full-fledged member since 1827. Huge posters in the streets and even in the Paris metro, unabashedly displaying the price of the jewel in the photograph, promotional campaigns on the Internet, a 17,89 % discount every July, 14th (official year and date of the French Revolution)—all of this shows a desire to leave the well-worn advertising paths in the jewelry sector, a desire that has been manifested in other ways, too, many of them just as heretical, such as opening a boutique sandwiched between a fast-food joint and a Benetton store (on the Champs-Elysées, but still…), or an offer for free credit.

For a long time, Skip followed the same advertising model as all its competitors: someone made a stain on a piece of clothing or a sheet, the housewife wailed and gnashed her teeth, and then remembered that she had a miracle product in the cupboard that would clean it all up. Stains were the enemy, and they were to be fought by any means and eliminated as quickly as possible. How to stand out in such a crowded and conformist market? By going at the problem from a different angle. "Dirt is good," said

Skip. You can't learn anything without getting a few stains, not cooking, not football, not painting: getting dirty is part of a child's life, and even an adult's. Whence the "splat" (the equivalent of the Nike "swoosh", a colored splash that now appears on all Skip packages) and also an ad campaign that showed not just kids grappling with tubes of paint but also a young woman dressed like a hippy with a long skirt and hair blowing in the wind, sitting on a trail bike and thus covered in mud, to whom the brand declares: "Don't worry anymore about getting your nicest clothes dirty."

In its big ad campaigns in the 1970s, the Beetle went against the grain of American automobile manufacturers, who sold the idea that a good car was a big one. "Think small," said Volkswagen, or else, "It's ugly, but it gets you there" (meaning: to the moon, an allusion to the number of miles a Beetle is capable of driving in the course of its lifetime).

From the very beginning, Diesel consistently built its identity on the non-conformism of its ad campaigns, which earned overwhelming approval all over the world from both the public and the profession. The trail had thus been blazed for L'Oréal when it launched the perfume " Diesel : Fuel for Life": the same anti-conformism forced the French group to break out of its habits by not using a celebrity spokesperson, avoiding overly glossy and flattering images, and instead using unexpected models, ironic layouts, and tongue-in-cheek taglines such as "Finally legalized" and "Only the Brave".

Dove made a complete about-face by leaving behind its focus on the product ("Our soaps contain 25 % skin cream") in favor of an approach that was revolutionary with respect to the advertising standards in the hygiene and beauty sector. Taking L'Oréal as its counter-model, the brand spear-headed a campaign against media stereotypes that went far beyond a mere commercial enterprise, shook up public perceptions, and even adopted positions (with the films "Brainwashing" and "Evolution") that one would be more likely to associate with an anti-advertising lobby group.

When it was launched in the United States, Absolut broke at once with all the norms of the vodka market and with the advertising norm for alcohol in general, which was very traditionalist at the time. Opting for a modern approach, Absolut took Andy Warhol up on his offer to paint the bottle in black on a yellow background. The saga began, and it continues to this day. Twenty years later, more than 500 artists have embroidered on the same theme, and the brand's advertising strategy, although it now includes cinema, publishing, and the web, remains the same. From the beginning, the brand's approach was clear: "Where others holler, we'll whisper." Yet another of the brand's advertising maneuvers, which consisted in putting the famous bottle in the background, where it is used as an accessory or decoration by a whole gallery of wildly creative characters, has helped transform those whispers into a buzz amplified by the internet, which obviously has been used to disseminate these new visuals, and even to put them on auction through Google.

We can thus see that choosing to break with advertising norms can help to construct a long-lasting brand identity, as is also demonstrated by Clinique and its decision—an unusual one in the cosmetics sector—never to show anything but its products, always framed by the same set of standard symbols and images.

The industry norm

An industry can change technical norms fairly quickly, as is currently the case in the electronics and automobile industries.

In electronics, the Blu-Ray format made inroads in the DVD market, spelling victory, at least in this area, for Sony over its competitor Toshiba.

The concerns surrounding global warming and pollution have gradually led governments to take various measures that are then passed on to producers and individuals. Some brands can get a jump on these trends: this is what Toyota managed so successfully to do with the Prius, a hybrid vehicle that created a new category of car. Others try to modify their identity by proclaiming their respect for the new norms, either through actions (Honda, with its Civic hybrid) or by claiming to be in line with the public's environmental concerns, as Mitsubishi did with the Outlander, "conceived and developed in the country of the Kyoto accords". Covered in dust for the needs of a press release, a finger traces the word "Respect" on the rear window, accompanied by four little flowers. When you consider that all the Mitsubishi outlanders have been hit in Europe with an environmental penalty of 750 euros, one wonders: respect for what? Who knows. One thing is clear, however, and that's Mitsubishi's wish to make known its awareness of and "respect" for the new norms in the automobile industry.

Nokia is justified in saying "Rewrite the rules": that's what made the Finnish brand. After having been a stationer and a tire, cable, television, rubber, and even toilet paper manufacturer, Nokia went into the portable telephone business in 1992 and made GSM the new digital norm worldwide.

Swatch completely changed the rules of the game for watches: beating the Japanese at their own quartz game, the brand flattened the product by assembling the parts of the electronic mechanism directly in the casing, which reduced the number of pieces and the time of manufacture. Instead of metal, they used colored plastic. Instead of the kind of heavy watch you solemnly give as a graduation present, they made ultra-light watches that you can change with the seasons or just because you feel like it. Instead of selling the watches at the little corner jewelry store, they made them available at sales points around the world. Instead of something serious, they created something fun, cool, and fashionable. All of this for just a few Swiss francs—or else for much more than a Seiko, if you're looking for a sold-out model. It would be hard to imagine a more revolutionary revolution.

FedEx has modified its industry's norms several times: by inventing the concept of "overnight delivery," by developing the "tracking" concept even before the name existed (each package is scanned at least six times during transport), by creating an automated call center so that clients could follow the progress of their packages, and then, starting in 1994, by offering the same service on the internet.

Virgin doesn't play by any of the rules that brands normally obey, including the rule of coherence: apart from its constant tendency to attack anything and everything that could be seen as a privilege or a norm, the brand doesn't seem to have any guideline except Richard Branson's desire to give his insights and wishes free rein.

New Balance, a brand that began by specializing in orthopedic shoes, opposes its three big competitors (Nike, Reebok, and Adidas) by positioning itself as a specialist, indeed almost as an artisan, of running shoes. No chance of getting caught up in the fashion whirlwind, no question of any fancy marketing campaigns or advertising barrages either—New Balance advertises mostly in sports publications and makes high-tech products for long-distance runners. Even its credo stands out from the competition: instead of the catchy "Just do it," a more tempered "Achieve New Balance," underwritten by media investments that amount to only 4 % of profits compared to 12 % for Nike, and budgets devoted to research and development rather than to large-scale sponsorships.

Among the numerous examples to be found in the automobile sector, the Fiat Panda is a good example of the benefits that a brand can derive from a rupture with the norms of the industry—especially when that rupture is the work of a brand whose identity has always obeyed the prevailing political, cultural, and social norms. The Panda is a little car designed by a big name in design, Giugiaro. The advertising for the car, like its design, "is born from the idea of transgression," say the brand's managers, because for the first time a little car is being sold not for its price or its low maintenance costs but because it's young, snazzy, and made for city life, for having fun, something the French tagline gets across pretty well by calling it the "car for making mischief".

The product norm

It would be tempting to think that the only option for a product that wants to stand out is to break with existing norms. This isn't quite true: unless you invent a three-sleeved coat, a high-heeled shoe with the heel in front, or a car without wheels, there are some products whose shape (at least for the moment) just can't be changed.

The color, however, the material, consistency, makeup, texture, and wrapping—all of these can vary in nearly infinite ways. That's what causes the product norm to change.

Before Eau Dynamisante by Clarins, nobody had been so bold as to sell a fragrance that was also a "treatment spray" and that came in a red bottle. Twenty-five years after the product was launched, the brand now gives it full-page advertisements and merely says: "The power of the red bottle."

Absolut was a Swedish vodka, which was totally outside the norm when it made its debut on the American market near the end of the 1970s. At the time, the norm was that vodka was Russian, or pretended to be. Ninety-nine percent of Americans drank vodka produced in their home country and crowned with various Polish or Russian names like Smirnoff, and 1% of vodka was really Russian: Stolichnaya. Nobody was willing to bet on the success of a Swedish vodka sold in a bottle shaped like a pharmaceutical flask. A similar approach (a bottle reduced to its purest essence, similar in shape to certain medicinal flasks), was adopted by Calvin Klein in the 1990s when it launched its ckBe perfume, with spectacular, but less enduring, results.

Between 1950 and 1970, Michelin revolutionized the tire market by equipping cars the world over with radial tires, forcing all of its competitors to imitate it.

A product innovation was at the origin of Uncle Ben's success: a manufacturing process that made the rice less sticky (an unbeatable argument in its favor, until the fashion shifted toward Asian rice, like sticky rice), plus an innovative package color (orange), a color that until then had never been seen on the food shelf. The same recipe worked wonders for Dyson, the vacuum cleaner without a bag. And Nike's empire, as we know, was based not on advertising but on the initial idea of sticking a thick rubber sole to the bottom of a jogging shoe, to give it shock-absorbent properties.

The brand norm

When a brand has made itself known by putting something new on the market, innovation is part of its history, that is to say its identity. If it forgets this, its identity is weakened—and it's always harder to crawl back up the slope than it is to slide down it. Bic was at the forefront of innovation with its pens, razors, and disposable lighters: once its innovations became rarer and less frequent, the brand had to move forward immediately with a big innovation program to have any chance of remaining the leader in each of its markets.

For several years, Sony, whose history and reputation are founded on innovation (the transistor in 1955, the Walkman, the Trinitron, the Playstation) seemed to have lost its touch. Its resurgence on the gaming and electronics market was established when Blu-Ray, a technology conceived in the firm's research and development labs, was adopted as the standard for high-definition films. Salomon burst onto the ski market in 1990 with its revolutionary monocoque technology, which rapidly propelled it to the number one position on the market. But the brand rested on its laurels and arrived on the parabolic ski market three years late, which nearly resulted in its missing the snowboard train entirely.

From its beginnings, and for a long time thereafter, Citroën was the embodiment of what it meant to break with the norm. Its founder began with "a motor and a patent on gears in a herringbone shape, a truly revolutionary technology: their special teeth made them work more smoothly, more quietly, and more efficiently."[20] The A-type, the 5 CV, front-wheel drive, the 2 CV, the DS, and the XM kept the flame of innovation alive, but then the wind changed direction. The flame looked like it might go out, advertising lit it up again in the 1980s, but advertising alone, as we know, can't mask a brand's weaknesses for long. Citroën's identity is no longer the same now that its name is attached to Peugeot's, as if, instead of joining forces, the two car makers had each lost half of their strength as a result of the merger. Innovation now comes from other quarters (or seems to): Renault, "a driving force of innovation for 100 years" in 1999, and then "automobile creator" since 2000, is in any event the leading French maker. Various maladroit confusions, such as the one generated by the uncanny similarities between the 106 and the Saxo, have helped neither Peugeot nor Citroën preserve their identity, and because of self-plagiarism and drops in price, Citroën's is now the weaker of the two.

The English weekly *The Economist* sticks to an editorial line that adheres closely to the norms established since the magazine's origins in 1843. The editor-in-chief's remarks testify to this: "Put the Iraq hostages on the front page? Too English! *The Economist* is an international magazine. It cannot express the British point of view." With on average two columns per subject, a single edition of 70 pages for the whole world, and a collective editorial policy, *The Economist* follows to the letter the rules of conduct that it has established for itself. This goes to show that its approach does indeed constitute a form of brand logic: "This 'community-based' organization is the best means of insuring cohesion and avoiding solo acts [in other words, the narcissistic tendencies of some journalists] that would erode our most precious asset: our brand."[21] The French daily *Le Monde* tends to fall into the opposite trap. But this daily has had a clear and strictly applied editorial line for ages, in other words its own norm, and the proof of this comes from Hubert Beuve-Méry, who founded the newspaper in 1944, and who is said to have told his troops at the time: "Make it bloody annoying."

The social or cultural norm

For a brand whose goal is to win the acceptance of the majority, or at least of a significant number of clients, it's impossible to ignore the prevailing social and cultural norms in the circles where one is operating.

It might even seem as if there's no other solution than to submit to them, and many brands do, explicitly or otherwise. This is the case with all brands that toe the politically correct line.

Many brands in all sectors—and American brands especially—are content to eat from the trough of normativity, with a little advertising sauce for flavor. The gruel has been reheated so many times that it doesn't taste the way it used to, and even Procter & Gamble has taken steps to spice things up a bit: a little Simpsons to sell Vizir, and fewer test tubes in the Ariel ads. But respect for the norm is still…the norm, and this is even truer when the norm is a law, and when that law is religious. After falling victim to a rumor that stated the logo blasphemed Islam when read backwards, Coca-Cola didn't hesitate. Now all of its ads in Egypt are preceded by the classic profession of faith: "There is no God but Allah and Mohammed is his prophet."

Some brands, on the other hand, charge headlong against the norm, first and foremost among them the ones that think a brand's goal is to do business, and that the only law out there is the law of profit and loss. Yes, said The Body Shop, a brand's goal is to make money, but no, profit isn't the only law. And The Body Shop said this loud and clear, especially when its founder, A. Roddick, had the floor: an activist through and through, she was at the cutting edge of what might be called ethical or humanitarian marketing, if such a thing really exists. In any event, rare was the cause The Body Shop wasn't somehow involved in, even if this meant overturning the norm stating that a brand at that time should worry about its own affairs without getting mixed up in social problems. In the 1980s, the brand sent its trucks out on the road adorned not with pretty faces but with declarations such as: "If you don't believe in education, try ignorance," or else used a plus-sized model accompanied by a message that thumbed its nose at the whole cosmetics industry: "Act natural. Enjoy your age." In the years since, Dove has taken up the same message.

However, other brands get around social and cultural norms without even challenging them: they simply invent new ones. That's what Sony did with the Walkman, which made a completely unprecedented behavior quite normal, namely doing two things at once: traveling, eating, writing, or jogging while listening to music. It's now hard to grasp just how bold this was, because the phenomenon has become "natural," unless we compare it with the kind of reactions that some cell phone users still elicit: someone who uses their cell phone in the bus or the restaurant, forcing everyone to overhear them, is likely to get a lot of dirty looks and nasty comments. In the same way, people were openly disapproving of the Walkman when it was first introduced. The disapproval was discreet, especially in Japan, but it was there. This was because one of the group's unwritten rules was being broken—the rule that makes it rude to engage in a private activity—like listening to music—in public.[22]

In another register, the same is true of Ikea, which introduced a new way of furnishing one's home or apartment, a simpler, more modern, and less conventional way, which relieved many young—and not so young—couples from the burden of having to look like they'd inherited or purchased "nice furniture" before they dared invite their family or neighbors for dinner.

In the United States in the 1960s and 70s, the norm where cars were concerned was to drive a big one, even a very big one. Going against the grain by proclaiming that "Small is beautiful," the Volkswagen Beetle became a friendly Tom Thumb in the land of giant cars. In the process, it got sucked into the hippy counter-culture. Its success was so great that thirty years later, when its descendant, the New Beetle, was put on the market, the great Peace and Love epic was used once again as a springboard, with just a few slight changes, as we saw earlier. In Germany, on the other hand, where the Beetle was never a counter-culture favorite, the New Beetle had a lot more trouble breaking into the market.

It can be very costly to violate cultural or social norms. Camay soap learned this the hard way in Japan[23] by trying to use the same advertising film there as everywhere else, with a script that had remained the same since 1958: a young woman in the bathtub covered in suds, and her husband, interested and curious, who comes to ask about her new perfume, whereupon she shows him the soap she's using. Procter & Gamble's only concession was to shoot the film with Japanese actors. Disaster! This time, Procter's tried-and-true recipe failed miserably. Any guidebook could have predicted this, even without the need to visit in person: because of the lack of space in the city and the tradition of public baths, apartments don't always have bathrooms, and those that do rarely possess big bathtubs. When they do, nobody washes themselves in them: you soap and rinse yourself *before* getting into a bath. Moreover, a Japanese husband would never barge into the bathroom while his wife was in there. Probably not in the West, either, but here we're used to advertisers taking liberties. In Japan, the film was taken at face value, and the public was deeply shocked. Camay's launch was a failure, as was the Japanese opening of Sephora ten years later, for similar reasons: the negligence and arrogance of a Western company that didn't take the trouble to look into its foreign clientele's habits. The LVMH group hadn't realized the degree to which the Japanese, who were accustomed to self-service for everyday goods but equally accustomed to extremely attentive service in the luxury sphere, would be taken aback by stores where you had to choose products sold at very high prices on your own, without any guidance or assistance.

It is thus better to be prudent with cultural norms. Today, one of ours, at least in the so-called "developed" countries, concerns environmental protection, and it would be unwise to risk violating it. Brands therefore go overboard in declaring their love for Gaia, the Earth Mother, which means they have to be very inventive to avoid being drowned out by the chorus of all these new little angels. Timberland has taken up the challenge, and, vaunting the eco-friendly qualities of its Earthkeepers (100 % organic cotton cloth, natural wax, 30 % recycled rubber for the soles), boasts: "Gear that refuses to walk all over the environment."

All the norms at once

Sony violated several norms at once in the 2000s with Playstation, going so far as to have Fifi—an improbable creature with a metallic voice—say totally iconoclastic things, such as "Humanity's great achievements leave me cold". The only thing that interests Fifi is virtual. She says: "I play, therefore I am," a declaration that raised the hackles of many who saw in such remarks an insidious means of inviting young people to flee from reality into the virtual world of video games, as if young Playstation aficionados needed any encouraging in this department.

But one has to be careful not to go too far. The Smart car almost died before it could be born, done in by too many violations of the norm: a new mode of production, a new distribution network, a revolutionary computer system, an advertising campaign that was anything but normal, and a completely unprecedented sort of car. The problems were legion. Faulty conception (a center of gravity placed too high—the Daimler-Chrysler engineers weren't used to building such small cars), delays in the product launch, astronomical prices, lack of inventory, a weak service network, and so on. On the other hand, it's true that Smart was attempting nothing less than to reinvent the automobile...

But things aren't always so difficult: it's possible to be an original and innovative brand where the product is concerned, to change the rules of the game, to have a strong identity, to adapt that identity to a new market, but without betraying it, and to get rewarded for doing so: Armani is the only European designer that's managed to have a significant presence in the US, where it competes successfully against Ralph Lauren (another very normative brand in its way, not a single hair is out of place in its impeccable reconstructions of the WASP milieu).

Armani owes much of its success to a strong identity that not only hasn't suffered from its efforts to fit into the American market, but has been able to assert itself even more clearly—cuts, material, color, everything has been thought through. The Americans don't like linen because it wrinkles? Instead of trying to explain to them, as any self-respecting Milanese person knows practically from birth, that linen is all the more beautiful for wrinkling well, Armani found linens that were more compatible with American prejudices in this area. They like blue and gray? It reworked its range of colors in these two tones. They have different builds than Europeans do? It adopted cuts to match, without compromising their style.

The same is true of Ikea, which sticks to its Scandinavian identity wherever the brand takes root, but which didn't hesitate to change the dimensions of its beds, couches, and kitchen furniture to suit local norms in the American market. Ikea even took the risk of scandalizing visual identity purists—and there are some very fierce ones within Ikea itself—by mixing the blue and yellow of the Swedish flag with the American stars and stripes.

As for Benetton, known for its controversial ads, and as a specialist in the art of delivering sharp blows to the soft underbelly of reigning mentalities, although it had to take a breather for a while because it had crossed the line one too many times, it periodically enters the fray again. Having begun by breaking with a technical norm that everyone has now forgotten (it began dying sweaters *after* they were made and not before, saving time and minimizing risks while sticking to fashion trends as closely as possible in an era in which it took its competitors eighteen months on average to go through the production cycle from factory to stores), the brand has preserved its tradition of disobedience. Having first shaken up the industry's habits, Benetton then transgressed the advertising norm: it put photos highlighting its products in stores, while in the press or elsewhere, it made declarations about all sorts of social or political subjects without any attempt to sell.

But the more norms one transgresses at the same time, the harder it is to keep transgressing in the long term. Take Yves Saint Laurent's Opium, for example, a brand in its own right that triggered a veritable revolution in the perfume sector in its day. At the time, everything looked new and very bold: the name, the stuff, the bottle, the allusion to the drug, of course, and the advertising. The scandal machine had to be turned on again several times; meanwhile, the brand's orientalism was wearing out. What to do? The brand resorted to nudity, which was gradually divested of all exoticism in spite of a few judiciously placed orchids. Thirty years after it appeared on the market, the Opium woman has lost just about all of her charm: made over, tamed, almost proper, she's lost her identity, and the perfume the cult status it had immediately conquered when it was released.

THE POSITIONS POLE

War and adventure movies have instilled in us the idea that position is sometimes the most precious indicator there is, even more precious than the name, for identifying a plane, a ship, or a person we know nothing about. "What is your position?" is the first thing they're asked when someone enters into contact with them. We do the same thing with our cell phones: Where are you? is often the first question we ask our interlocutors.

In the same way, the Positions pole (which, let it be noted, has nothing to do with "positioning" in the marketing sense of the term) consisting in asking: what is the brand's position?

There are several ways to answer this question.

The first is direct. Some brands answer by saying: "This is what I am." These answers differ, they can be quantitative or qualitative ("I'm the number one insurance company in South America" or "I'm the best sparkling mineral water in Europe").

The second way of answering is a sort of response by proxy: the brand doesn't say "I'm this or that" but "My consumer is like this or that". Nothing shows that consumers are on the inside and not the outside of brands better than this tendency toward total identification, which leads some brands to declare: "I am what my consumer is."

The third way of answering the question "What is your position?" is to say "It depends on yours". In the case of brands, the two respective positions occupied by the brand and its consumers have to be defined, explicitly or implicitly. As we'll see, this is a very common scenario, but let's look at the other two answers first.

"I am..."

There are many examples of brands that not only respond directly to the question "What is your position?" but also make a point of displaying it openly:

- Hermès is a "contemporary artisan since 1837";

- BASF is "the chemical company";

- Breguet is "the innovator";

- Wikipedia is "the free encyclopedia."

Sometimes, the approach is slightly indirect. The consumer has to figure out, for example, that Glenfiddich has a "pioneering spirit" because it's a Scottish brand. Or that Patek Philippe is a family, because the brand always uses the "we" pronoun. Or, even more indirect, but not very subtle, that Rolex is the king of watchmakers, because the brand bears a crown and awards aristocratic bona fides ("Every crown is an achievement"). Shell no longer puts a tiger in your engine—it has become a coach ("Let's go"). Esprit invites everyone to make a wish—the brand is a good fairy. Conversely, Diesel is a wicked imp ("Be stupid").

Most of the time, however, brands don't use such explicit language. Their position of self-affirmation is stated via a declaration about general values, like a philosopher or a thinker whose reputation for rock-solid reasoning would earn him the right to speak up in public and to be instantaneously respected. Hiding behind a statement such as "Entertainment is a vital need" (Vivendi) is a position of authority, in the sense that one says of someone: "He's an authority in his field." Vivendi's declaration amounts to saying: "I'm an authority in the entertainment domain, and I speak to you from the summits of this uncontested position."

All brand discourse that's built on the "X is Y" model stems from the same principle, whatever kind of guise it's wrapped in—a simple one ("Skincare for Life", Nivea) or a more solemn one ("The best feelings are the ones we share", Total). Some limit themselves to general statements that nobody would dream of finding objectionable (see above), while others are more imperious ("Do the don'ts", Juicy Couture). It's obviously impossible to utter such words except from a dominant position—and here the Oscar goes (for the moment, that is) to Volvo, which, when in 2008 it decided to award the prize for "Ecological Brand of the Year" to Patagonia, set itself up as the authority in all matters ecological, entitled to hand out blame and praise.

Other brands say what they are without necessarily entrusting the task of saying so to their promotional campaigns: "We are soccer," said Adidas just before the 1998 World Cup, and not without reason: Adidas invented cleats, and the brand's history has long been closely tied to the history of soccer, in a more legitimate way than Nike's.

Nivea's purifying patches almost never got marketed by Beiersdorf, which thought the Japanese-born product too "brutal" (it has to be pulled off the skin like a Band-Aid to remove the blackheads), in other words "not soft enough for a brand that owes its fame to the smoothness of its signature cream". Nivea defines itself as a soft brand.

By the same token, at Nestlé it's acknowledged that "Ricoré is a gentle brand." Brandt is a "masculine" brand, "because of its strength and solidity."

There are cases where the brand's self-description is baffling, as when it consists in a tautological self-reference of the type "I am this," the "this" in question consisting in a melting pot of words and images generated by the brand's advertisements. This was the case in France with Coca-Cola's post-war "*Coca-Cola, c'est ça*" campaign ("This is Coca-Cola"), and with McDonald's ("*Ça se passe comme ça chez McDonald's*") ("This is how it happens at McDonald's"), or with Cadbury ("This is Cadbury"). When the images in question draw on the same stock of advertising clichés, the risk is obviously that identity will be diluted in a "this" that equals a "nothing."

"You are…"

A consumer is what's left of a human being after marketing has sucked most of its brains out—proving that "savages" are not the only ones to be adept at head shrinking—which is why I use the word "consumer" with repugnance, and only because it's convenient. But the logic can be taken still further, as some marketers have shown by isolating a "shopper" inside the consumer. All that was left after the first brain-shrinking operation was tiny little pea, but now that pea has been shrunk down to pinhead size.

The brands that define themselves via consumers reduced to "shoppers" obviously don't have a very rich or wide basis for their identity. Sometimes that basis amounts to using a marketing segmentation provided by some research firm. Indeed, the head shrinkers delight in a good segmentation, which consists in forcing consumers into a few little boxes that are given supposedly evocative names. To date, the race to achieve the smallest possible unit of meaning appears to have been won by Ariel Essential at its coming out party in 2000: it defined its consumers as "people who are in a good mood so long as they can put on nice, clean clothes," which meant the brand could promise "more vitality" if they did their laundry with Ariel.

Fortunately, some brands have a slightly broader, yet nonetheless precise, vision of things.

New Balance, for example, reckons that its clients "are athletic, not fashion victims, and not adolescents but in the 25–60 range".

Quicksilver is "the boardriding company," "the brand for people who slide on boards," specifies the CEO, a definition imitated by Rossignol, which presents itself as "the brand of people obsessed with sliding."

Olay announced the opening of OlayforYou.com with a huge "You" superimposed on the face of a woman sitting in front of her computer, her face framed inside the central "o".

Patek Philippe is aiming at clients who are fortunate enough to think in terms of the family inheritance, staging a conversation between a son and his father, who declares "You never actually own a Patek Philippe, you just look after it for the next generation."

Yves Saint-Laurent was even clearer, declaring: "Rive Gauche isn't a perfume for wall-flowers," and Azzaro stated that one of its colognes was for "men who like women who like men." The watchmaker IWC is just as clear, showing close-ups of watches "made for navigators". Likewise, Bretling offers "instruments made for professionals," while Girard Perregaux presents itself as a watchmaker "for the few since 1791". Alfa Romeo describes Alfa 147 owners thus: "You have a sense of beauty." And Timberland's consumers have no trouble seeing themselves in the declaration: "Nature needs heroes."

A brand is therefore very much capable of defining itself through its consumers, with the caveat that when the consumer changes, the brand's identity does too, or risks doing so. This is why some brands, "hijacked" by a clientele that wasn't included in the marketing plan, do all they can to control the damage inflicted by these unexpected detours. Petit Bateau never complained about the fact that mothers started wearing the tee-shirts that were in theory for their daughters, and for good reason: the brand itself had carefully organized this phenomenon by inundating the editorial staffs of the top fashion magazines with the tee-shirts in question. But Timberland, for example, wasn't at all pleased when big city fashion victims started to buy their lumberjack boots, nor did Helly Hansen jump for joy when its down jackets, intended for mariners, found their way into the sketchiest neighborhoods in great numbers. Lacoste was no less dismayed when youth from the poorest Parisian suburbs started to chase after anything with a little crocodile on it in the late 1990s. Though one of the brand's top-level executives declared that the brand was "a sign of transcultural and trans-generational integration that originates in sports—a world where there's no such thing as a ghetto" and that Lacoste was "proud to cut across class and culture divides and to clothe everyone from truck drivers to the King of Spain," the security guards that suddenly appeared at the doors of Lacoste stores suggested just how overjoyed the brand really was about welcoming this unexpected influx of new clients. And yet fifty years earlier, Levi's had shown that a hundred-year-old brand with a strong identity and a product with cult status could get a second wind when, without any advance warning, rebellious youngsters got ahold of it and made it their own. On the other hand, it's true that the rebellious generation in question was led by the likes of James Dean, Marilyn Monroe, and Marlon Brando...

The misadventures of Levi's provide a good illustration of how much brand identity owes its consumers. Many analysts have noted that Levi's resurgence is due to the fact that the Baby Boomers bought into the brand, and sociologists have added that its recent problems can be blamed (as I noted earlier) on the following generation's refusal to wear the same uniform as its parents, so as to adopt something new and unique—rapper's track suits, "carpenter" pants, or baggy jeans worn low on the hips, for example.

Perrier's misadventures offer another example of the difficulties encountered by brands when their identity is embodied by a "target" on the decline: in the United States, the golden boys of the late 1980s propelled Perrier to success, but then played a role in the brand's collapse, just as big a role as the Benzene scandal of 1990. Anyone who gets catapulted to the top of the heap by the spirit of the times can be sure of only one thing: that the same spirit will bring them back down again just as fast as they went up in the first place.

Harley-Davidson is another one of these brands that is heavily (too?) dependent on their consumers. The products are said to lack technological sophistication, and thus the brand resides entirely in its image, which is itself a reflection of the bikers who choose Harley-Davidson. Provided people keep wanting to be like those bikers, the brand is safe, but should the Hell's Angels style ever go out of fashion, Harley-Davidson could easily go with it.

"We are..."

A brand is an interface with the consumer, and thus its Position, as we've just seen, can be either its own or the consumer's. The third possibility involves respective positions.

This isn't as complicated as one might think at first glance, and at the same it's absolutely crucial, if we think about the positions we all occupy, consciously or unconsciously, in our personal interactions.

Let's take the case of Mrs. Miller and her grandson Ben, who is four years old. Mrs. Miller has her own identity and Ben has his. But that doesn't tell us anything about the place that each grants the other, about their respective positions. If Ben is very dear to his grandmother, she'll put him first no matter what. Let's say one of her friends calls her while she's playing with Ben—she'll cut the conversation short and hang up at once if Ben looks the least bit impatient, or even before. If, on the other hand, the friend in question is dearer to her heart than her grandson (anything is possible), she'll send him off to watch a DVD while she chats with her friend. For his part, the young Ben may love his grandmother more than anyone, but on the other hand his favorite may also be his mother, or his little brother, or his best friend.

The Palo Alto Group spent a lot of time studying the role of positions, within families for example, and their analysis forms the basis of the psychotherapies they use. Everything is based on the twofold concept of symmetry and complementarity introduced in 1936 by the anthropologist G. Bateson in his study of a New Guinean tribe, the Latmul, about whom he wrote his book *Naven*.[24]

All relationships are either symmetrical or complementary:

- In a symmetrical relationship, the partners behave as if they were on the same level: each takes turns leading, taking the initiative in conversation, etc. They arrange things so as to maintain this equality.

- In a complementary relationship, the partners are in an unequal position with respect to each other: if one is authoritative, the other is submissive; if one gives, the other receives, etc. They arrange things so as to maintain the difference that is at the basis of their relationship.

In principle, it is no better to establish symmetrical relationships than it is to establish complementary ones: what's important is that the partners agree on their respective positions. In the context of the family therapy sessions conducted at the Mental Research Institute in Palo Alto, this was rarely the case. By dint of observing the blockages and dysfunction afflicting these families, D. Jackson, P. Watzlawick, and their colleagues arrived at a few basic postulates, the first of which being that there is a basic unit underlying all human relations, the dyad, in other words the interaction between two people (this can be extended to two groups of people).

Dyads (for example, the relationship between husband and wife, master and disciple, business and union, or between two nations, two religions, etc.) are systems. A brand is also a dyad, in other words, the result of a relationship generated by and between two partners, in this case the company that owns the brand and the public. This relationship tends toward some kind of equilibrium and is always being readjusted so as to maintain that equilibrium in spite of the turbulence that threatens to throw it off balance. This dyad is obviously incredibly complex: when you think about how complex even a relationship reduced to two individuals can be (a father and son, a wife and a husband), you get an idea of the devilish complexity of the relationship between a brand and its consumers, two "partners" who are as dissimilar as can be from the perspective of size, makeup, organization, and their interest in maintaining or putting an end to the relationship.

We can also see that whatever brands say is said against a complementary background rather than a symmetrical one: the one looks to sell, the other sometimes feels like buying, or not. This is something we'll come back to, since it's closely involved in the Relations pole.

For the moment, let's note that there is a typology of dyads: six in all, of which, for clarity's sake, I'll cite only the first four.

Examples of the first four dyads are everywhere around us: (1) a mother and her child are in the most typical complementary relationship; (2) two high school friends, in the same class, with the same grades and from the same socio-economic background, have a symmetrical relationship; (3) two Japanese families who meet for the first time are in symmetrical competition for the inferior position, as the greeting ceremony and the subtle exchange of bows suggests; (4) two hockey teams competing on the ice for Olympic gold are in a competitive, symmetrical relationship for the superior position.

A remark: dyads three and four are mostly encountered in personal relationships between sellers and clients, and they can become pretty perverse. Dyad four, for example, is a specialty of "in" fashion brands, usually located between the upper section of the middle range and the lower regions of the luxury sector, and underwritten by women's magazines. The relationships that spring up between sellers and "fashion victims" are worth their weight in caviar, each doing his (or her) best to outdo the other for the superior position.

As for dyad three, it can be seen in the context of seller-client relations, but in just about all sectors, between a buyer who's a little unsure of himself and a shrewd salesperson. The first admits that he has no idea what he's looking for, and the second, to put him at his ease, then says that she herself has trouble making sense of the complex offers available from the various manufacturers.

But it's clear that these two types of attitude can only occur in certain types of personal interaction, and not in a brand's global behavior vis-à-vis its consumers. That's why the most frequent dyads in the world of brands are dyads one and two: symmetry and complementarity, both stable, at least for a time, until changes in the market, the brand, or the consumers lead to a shift in equilibrium.

Stable complementarity

In launching the first iMac in 1998, Apple defined two mutually complementary positions: one for its consumers (children impatient to "play on the internet", who are invited to "Plug and play"), and the other, of course, for itself (the adult who satisfies the child's whims). The brand occupies the position of superiority.

Starbucks initiated Americans into the mysteries of coffee, making it the master guiding hordes of consumer-apprentices; here, too, the brand occupies the position of superiority. After a long study, Hewlett-Packard discovered that the brand's values made it a "mentor".

By the same token, there is a relationship of complementarity between the perfume "J'adore" and the adoring fans of the Dior brand, who jump at the chance to spend bundles on tee-shirts emblazoned with the words "J'adore Dior". What could be more logical? In French, the name "Dior" combines "god" ("*dieu*") and "gold" ("*or*"). And as the French say, one adores only God, who is always surrounded by a golden halo, like the blond bombshell Charlize Theron, who was hired for the campaign but is so suffused in golden light that unless you read her name on the posters it's sometimes impossible to recognize her: the holy image is literally blinding. All one can do is worship it.

When a brand has institutional pretensions, it establishes a complementary relationship in which it occupies the "superior" position: Danone, for example, with the Danone Institute for Health, which issues proclamations as if it were a Ministry—whence the need to balance out this lofty stance with brand advertising in the narrower sense, so as to be on equal footing with the consumer.

By the same token, Total says, "For you, our energy is limitless", and McDonald's, "We love to see you smile."

The role reversal suggested by "At Nestlé, the baby is CEO," is another way of showing that for some brands, the only possible position is to act on the assumption that the client is king.

Stable symmetry

Gap doesn't want to be seen as a "style prescriber. Our brand celebrates individualism, and all our campaigns show people wearing Gap clothing in their own way. Gap adapts to the individual styles of its clients." For several years, UBS has been closing its campaigns with a simple "You and Us".

With the declaration "Imagination walks," Camper sets up a mirroring relationship between itself and its consumers, who also have lots of imagination, this common trait bringing them closer to the brand.

Cacharel's perfume Anaïs Anaïs has long based its identity on the double mirroring of positions: the faces of two young girls leaning toward each other, so similar that they sometimes looked to be the same (and sometimes they were): a symmetrical, almost twinned, position. And then the other symmetrical position occupied by the young girls for whom the image is intended, and who are also absorbed in the kind of narcissistic introspection so typical of early adolescence.

That said, although the life expectancy of a dyad can be pretty long, it's not eternal. There always comes a time when it has to be changed, and this moment is full of danger.

Anaïs Anaïs fell off the list of best-selling perfumes when it abandoned its mirroring and the absolute symmetry that went with it: a young girl, all alone, spoke in the brand's name for the first time. By moving from "We" to the "I" disguised behind a smiling declaration, the model looking right in our eyes ("One day, tenderness will move the world"), the brand threw its positions off balance and profoundly transformed its identity, which started to look too much like that of its competitors to maintain the differential gap without which no major brand can survive for very long.

Passing time tends to shift the equilibrium of all dyads. Now that Starbucks has initiated its consumers, it has to change its position, since they've all become connoisseurs, or at least coffee buffs.

When the profane become initiates, they leave their teachers behind: they need a new one, or maybe they don't need one at all anymore, or just don't want one. By the same token, children eventually grow up, and rebels have to choose between shaping up and being marginalized: sooner or later, Apple will have to change its position and stop treating its clients like the blindly faithful members of a sect. For the moment, it's doing the opposite, hardening its position of superiority, and discarding the cool big brother role in favor of an arrogance and an imperialism that have drawn a good deal of criticism, some of it from people who had been big fans of the company, or, worse still, loyal clients.

To correct this kind of damaging trend (which is always possible when you get carried away by stunning successes like the iPod, the iPhone, and the iPad), Nivea has been very careful to balance out its corporate campaign on the theme of "beauty", where it is the only one to have a voice, with various changes to its website, which offers a forum for the public's multiple voices.

THE RELATIONS POLE

There's a world of difference between what brands say about the topic of relations, and what the public thinks. In general, brands tell marvelous tales that the public listens to with an air of distraction, or skepticism—or that it doesn't listen to at all.

Take a word like "authenticity":[25] brands love it (along with a couple of others, like "trust", "convenience", "friendliness", "transparency"—but the list is too long to run down it here). For some brands, "authenticity" is so important that, to hear them talk, you would think that everything they think and do is guided by it, and comes back to it like a touchstone for figuring out what is and isn't valuable—this is the case at Philips, for example.

The logic these brands are using looks airtight: young people, in particular, want more authenticity (or more convenience, more transparency, etc.). We're going to do all we can to give it to them, and to say so. They'll appreciate the effort, and so they'll be loyal to us. QED.

But now listen to these remarks from a young English surfer, T. Carr, age fifteen:

> I won a competition which was sponsored by Coca-Cola and I thought at the time that that was a bit weird. For me, there has to be a clear link between the brand and the person or event they're sponsoring. I mean, it's nice to come out of the water and have a can of Coke, because it's fizzy and it gives you an energy boost, but what's the relation between Coke and surfing? It doesn't make much sense to me. I won a board which had the Coke logo on it; it was a good board but the logo put me off a bit. It's not a proper surf logo, really, and so I was advised to sell it. I was told it would be really popular with tourists, but for me, it just wasn't authentic. Still, I guess that for Coke they wanted to get more involved with the coolness of surfing, and it was certainly good that they helped make the competition happen. A much better example of good sponsorship, I think, is when Playstation sponsored the first local surfing competition at night. In my mind, there's a good fit between them, because of all the lights and special effects.[26]

To paraphrase an old Ford advertising campaign, what's important isn't what you say but what you do. If what you do reveals an authenticity that's different from the one you're claiming to display—an authentic commercial enterprise, and not an authentic interest in surfing—the airtight logic I mentioned above comes back at you like a boomerang.

This kind of misunderstanding is a constant between brands and the public, and it's always the same: it consists in hiding the foundational relation, the commercial one, the one that all the others are based on, and in stacking on top of it everything consumers "expect" (as if it were obvious that they're all expecting, hoping for, or wanting something): complicity, warmth, feeling, whatever you want. And then in hoping that everyone is happy.

Have you ever tried to build a house of cards? If so, has it ever occurred to you to pull out the ones at the bottom and to hope that the rest will just keep floating in the air?

The relations that a brand has with its consumers are just as fragile, first of all because they start by denying the existence of the foundation they're built on, in other words by acting as if a market transaction wasn't the ultimate goal of the relationship.

And there's a second reason for that fragility too: it's impossible to establish an utterly neutral relationship. As soon as we make contact with someone or something—and this is as true for brands as it is for places, events, or people—provided we attribute some slight degree of importance to the encounter, even a fleeting importance, we see it as being positive or negative. The attraction or aversion, sympathy or antipathy that we feel are immediate and hard to control, and psychology and cognitive science are finding new evidence of this every day.

Obviously, in the case of brands, only one of these two possibilities can arise. If the first impression is chilly, if subsequent impressions suggest a distant, aggressive, or arrogant attitude, the brand is in danger. If the first impression is non-existent, that's hardly any better. The range of possible relations between brands and consumers is therefore restricted to the "positive" side of things on the spectrum of human relations, whence the emergence of "lovemarks".[27]

It often follows from this that the only way of addressing the question of relations consists in drawing up a long list of good qualities. In practice, however, the vocabulary used is boiled down to just a few words:

■ McDonald's is always trying to elicit the same feel-good emotions with its "We love to see you smile" or "I'm loving it" slogans.

■ Brandt hopes to "establish a strong affective bond" with women by telling them, "It's good to be able to count on Brandt".

■ On the other hand, with its website Dior doesn't want "to become a "girlfriend" brand for web surfers";

■ Nestlé declares that "Ricoré is a gentle, nice brand. Ricoré and its consumers have almost a loving relationship with each other".

But these lists of values and qualities aren't very useful because almost all brands use the same ones, which doesn't really help them stand out from one another. Who doesn't want to have warm, trusting, close, loyal, and solid relations with their clients?

It's much more useful to ask how the relations a brand has with its consumers are structured over the years. And they're always structured, but at a very deep level, which explains why it's sometimes so difficult to get them to change. In fact, it's almost impossible when you don't know what relational model is at work beneath the deceptively smooth surface of things. Many focus groups are disappointing because the consumers, who are put in a totally artificial situation (being told to talk for three hours straight about a beer brand they've never heard of before tends to leave most people speechless), just end up repeating over and over again the words and phrases that marketing has taught them to use. Since they've agreed to be there, and since they'll be getting a check on the way out, they play along and talk, even if they don't have anything to say. No surprise, then, that the result is a litany of prefabricated phrases, mirroring those the group leader initially suggested. No matter how hard he tries, when the leader asks "What is your relationship with this brand?" he always gets the same answers, whether the subject is shoes, canned soup, or nightgowns.

A list of words isn't good for much of anything. On the other hand, two very simple models for analyzing relationships, developed by the Palo Alto Group, can help us understand the way brands and consumers relate to each other:

■ the first involves teasing out the implications of the famous principle which states, to paraphrase the words of P. Watzlawick, that "every communication has two aspects, relation and content, such that the first always encompasses the second";

■ the second involves figuring out how to use another principle, which states that "every relationship conforms to one of two models: play or ritual".

Relation and content

The relations that a brand has with its consumers, whether they are regular or occasional consumers, is crucial because it is what gives meaning to communication content. And as we've seen, everything about a brand is communication.

This shouldn't be taken to mean that relations are more important than content—in certain instances, a brand can have excellent relations with its consumers without this in the least guaranteeing the success of a new venture. Everyone loved Bic, but that wasn't enough to ensure the success of Bic perfumes. Conversely, a brand can have stormy relations with its clients without immediately going bankrupt, as is often the case in the airline industry (did someone say Ryanair?).

As always, it's important to guard against all kinds of extremism.

And yet, it's true that relationships are fundamental. There is no better proof of this than Coca-Cola's success: it has little to do (and never has, if we go by the fact that the product itself has never been exclusive or rare) with the drink itself. Some psychologists explain that Coca-Cola sells because of the ties between generations and also the ties binding the world's cultures together. This quasi-spiritual bond means that Coca-Cola transcends time and space and thus becomes a part of humanity's heritage, supposedly embodying a living harmony among peoples all over the planet.

The Club Med "product" was behind the brand's initial success, but it must be noted that a certain kind of relationship was built into the brand from the beginning, and was clearly just as responsible. It was that relationship that people were seeking from the Club, otherwise they would have gone to the neighboring hotel in Djerba or Agadir, which also offered room, board, and the same climate, sometimes for less and in a more luxurious environment. Of course, the "everything included" formula was attractive, but others imitated it. What they never imitated was the system of G.O.'s (Gracious Organizers) and G.M.'s (Gracious Members), and village chiefs, and the ties that were formed among them.

When the New Beetle was launched, Volkswagen's marketing department deliberately chose to use the brand's traditional language ("honest, unpretentious, and original") so as not to risk moving away from "what's fundamental, that is to say the emotional ties that exist between the Beetle and its fans."

Legend has it that the Queen of England was given a new Barbour jacket when she asked the company to repair the one she had. "Thank you," she replied, "but repair the other one anyway, I'm very attached to it." So attached, that she probably didn't even notice that a Barbour is heavy, that it can sometimes be hard to get rid of its smell, and that in the "warm, light, and waterproof jacket" category there are more advanced and less expensive products out there. But the relationship is stronger than the content: walks in the forest, horseback rides, fishing and hunting trips, real or imaginary, have settled on the Barbour brand like a patina in the collective memory.

The brands that have managed to generate this "security blanket" effect seem to have scaled the heights of the brand loyalty Olympus that everyone has been striving to reach for some time.

But it may be in the food sector that the role of relations is most noticeably dominant with respect to content (the product). The whole sector, or just about, is under the sign of the "nourishing" relation, that is to say the maternal figure and her various substitutes (in that he represents tradition, a doting grandfather can easily stand in for the mother, as in the ads for Werther's Originals). What this means is that it's practically impossible to be a food brand without establishing emotional relations, even if you can point to concrete qualities that truly distinguish your product from the competition.

Regarding this mothering relationship, there is a more commanding relation at work, and we find it across every product category. It consists in giving orders, or if not orders at least advice, encouragement, suggestions, in short, in reorienting behaviors, or at least in suggesting that this might be possible, even desirable. The examples are legion: "Never Hide" (Ray-Ban), "You can" (Canon), "Be like no other" (Vaio/Sony), "Take care" (Garnier), "Overcome the introvert inside you" (nikewomen.com), "Express yourself" (Lavazza)—descendants all, it would seem, of Nike's famous "Just do it," itself the inheritor of an advertising language that always uses the imperative to make its point ("Careful, Madam! You're starting to look a little plump! Use Amiral soap, with its special secret ingredient, and you will remain forever svelte and elegant."[28]).

The latter example shows that although content (in this case the soap, or the soap brand) is interchangeable, the relation that envelops it is always more or less stable, and oscillates between two main options: coax like Mother or command like Father.

Play and ritual

Advertising is often in charge of determining the kind of relations that the brand wants to create with its consumers. It can do this in explicit or implicit fashion.

Explicit: Brother's taglines ("At your side") or Epson's ("Who understands you better than Epson?"[29]). Implicit : the relation expressed by Nestlé in its logo, a nest with a bird and two little hatchlings.

But sometimes it's a combination of reflection and a more global approach that determines the kind of relations that the brand wants to have with its consumers. Boots triggered a veritable revolution just before the 2000s by putting a Health & Beauty Experience salon on the second floor of the High Kensington Street store in London. It offered 44 different services, from skin cleansing and laser hair removal (at prices scarcely higher than those of a traditional wax) to tattoos. Because of this increasingly holistic approach to health, which now includes well-being, everything has changed at the legendary British store. "Our mission has always been to help people feel better. Now, we're seeking to help them be in the best shape possible," is the word at Boots. The pharmacy even set up programs like the Smoking Cessation Program and Boots Dental. Preparatory appointments for patients who haven't seen a dentist in a long time and non-profit activities completed the panoply of initiatives set up to get across this broadening in the relations that Boots intends to establish with its clients.

This example is symptomatic of the *play* that a brand introduces into its relations with the consumer in order to freshen and liven them up. Thanks to the effect of surprise, a slight disorientation, a new space, new products, or new habits, established ritual is disrupted.

All *true* changes in "concept," that is to say those that aren't limited to choosing a new carpet or some fashionable furniture, are forms of play. They amount to shifts in brand identity, and this shift is expressed by introducing play into the (too) well-oiled relational ritual. We see this in the "retailtainment" trend that started in the United States, in which the resources of showbiz are used to enliven stores and entertain the consumer. In every instance what's going on is quite different from selling: it's a matter of building a relationship with the client that isn't just about selling.

There are also cases in which play is an intrinsic part of brand identity, as is the case at Diesel and Google (the playful visual riffs on the logo). But if it becomes the rule, the game no longer leads to play (that is, to space, movement) but paradoxically turns into *ritual*.

I don't mean to imply that the one is better than the other: brands need both.

Weight Watchers is a highly ritualized brand, like Avon and Tupperware, and without using advertising but simply through meetings or sales in the home. Obao is trying to come back after a long hiatus by offering its "beneficial Far Eastern rituals" on the internet, and it has organized its site around the visual rite that consists in opening double sliding doors. In their way, Ikea and Starbucks are also ritualized brands: only initiates know how an Ikea store is organized, that you have to note the reference number of the furniture with little pencils and sheets that are available all over the store, or else you can't pick them up in the aisles where they're stored lying flat in big cardboard boxes, which you have to collect yourself before going to the register. A client who walks into a Starbucks for the first time is taken aback when someone asks for his name and what he wants to drink: the menu is made up of bizarre names, he doesn't know what he wants right away, nor that he has to pay before being served, nor that they've asked for his name (first name, not last) in order to write it on the cardboard cup that's waiting for him at the other end of the counter. If he becomes a regular client, he will be expecting (among other things) these same familiar rituals, and through them he will become part of the Starbucks community.

Beer is a ritual that is celebrated in pubs and bars. Guinness understood this so well that it sells precisely that: an Irish pub, people who get together there to drink a beer, be together, play pool and darts, sing and chat. In partnership with the Irish Pub Company, and others, Guinness sells ritualized Irish conviviality, with beer at the center.[30]

It took some time for Orangina to turn one of the product's slight handicaps into an advantage: the bottle has to be shaken so that the pulp mixes in with the drink, or else it stays on the bottom. Then came the "Shake me, shake me!" advertising campaign, which is ongoing and has been taken up by Orangina Rouge. Orangina's brand has become ritualized.

Some brands have never had to go through the play stage to establish a ritual. Estée Lauder, for example, is an extremely ritualized brand, which never strays from its own rules. Rolex is the same, as is L'Oréal Paris.

Rolex, however, regularly introduces a bit of play into its advertising ritual (going so far, in a caption accompanying a photo of singer Diana Krall, as to brandish the following unexpected words: "Breaking the rules"), while Estée Lauder and L'Oréal Paris, at the two ends of the beauty market, will suffer sooner or later, and probably sooner than later, from having remained locked up in their own ritual for too long.

From time to time, there *must* be play. In general, brands don't acknowledge this until they have their backs against the wall because play brings disorder and they still think that disorder is a form of evil that has to be combated by all possible methods. Once they have realized that disorder is also the only means of injecting life into a system heading for sclerosis, as is the case with any excessively ritualized system, they may give in a little more willingly.

THE PROJECTS POLE

All of our actions have a goal, whether we're always aware of it or not. We are what we are projecting to do or to be.

There's nothing surprising in that: Charles Taylor reminds anyone who may have forgotten that "in order to have a sense of who we are, we have to have a notion of how we have become, and of where we are going," identity being "the direction our lives are moving in or could move in."[31]

The Projects pole is less a pole of things gained than of things intended. What's been gained already is static, while intention is dynamic. I'm not only the sum of what I've already been until now, I'm above all whatever I have the intention of becoming. Everything I do, all my acts of communication (words, gestures, looks, actions) express this intention, sometimes without my being aware of it. The same is true for other people, to whom I ascribe various intentions, real or imaginary.

That's why we never get very far (usually not much farther than our name) when we seek to answer the question "Who am I?" right off the bat, at least so long as we look for the answer in the rearview mirror. But if we look ahead, things get clearer.

The same is true of brands: we can answer the identity question by trying to figure out their intentions, their projects, their stakes, their values, their beliefs, in short, whatever drives them forward, whatever motivates them.

This may be even more blatantly true for brands than for people, because all of a brand's actions have a clear objective, timeframe, and budget, which is rarely the case with individuals. Paradoxically, even when it doesn't do what it was planning to do, a brand's action is always deliberate. If it's necessary to divert budgetary resources to a promotional campaign in order to counter a competitor's campaign, the brand does so, reluctantly, perhaps, but deliberately and consciously, with a precise aim in mind.

Of course, the word Projects is both too broad and too narrow for everything that I'm trying to fit into it, but let's simplify things once again.

And, first off, allow me to note that deciding to initiate a project happens in three stages:

- I'm in state A.

- In light of vision, value, stake, belief, or conviction X…

- …my project consists in attaining state B.

Which, in the language of companies and brands, could take the following form:

- I'm number four in my sector.

- In light of the projection that in a few years there will be room for only three brands…

- ...my project consists in moving from number four to number three over the coming year, and in climbing up another rung the year after.

Or else:

- I'm a bank with a solid position in the European market, but this market is extremely crowded.
- In light of my conviction that the best possibilities for developing a bank like mine are in South America...
- ...my project consists in becoming the first European bank in South American within three years.

Or else:

- I'm an organic food brand.
- In light of my refusal to pollute the environment with plastic packaging...
- ...my project consists in looking for the least toxic and the least expensive "paper and glass" solutions out there.

Club Med was born of exactly this kind of logic. At the end of World War II, Gérard Blitz went to meet with Gilbert Trigano in order to buy tents to create a vacation enclave in the Mediterranean. "The world as it is disagrees with me," he said. "I want to create another one. There's much to be done, society has changed, and now it's up to us to make it evolve. You can help me offer new vacations at great prices to people who have been dreaming of nothing else."[32]

A brand has to be moving to have an identity, and this movement takes the form of a project, because if it's not moving forward, it's going backwards, and if it stays in one place, it's also going backwards. The only choice it has is to keep projecting itself into the near or distant future. It follows that the Projects pole is structured around two of the three stages in project development:

- stage one belongs to the Positions pole: "I am" (or else "You are" or "We are") in such and such a "position" or state.
- stage two is the motivation stage: in the name of what will the project take shape? In light of what stake? What values? What vision of the future? What belief? What convictions?
- stage three is the definition and kicking off of the project itself.

In daily life, it sometimes takes us less than a second to go from stage one to stage three. In the life of brands, it obviously takes longer.

Let's now move directly to stages two and three, since the first, as I've said, corresponds to the Positions pole.

In the case of Karcher, for example, things are clear. At stage two, we have a brand whose motivation is to put "its expertise and savoir-faire to work renovating national heritages." It proclaims this at stage three by saying, with a little wink, "For us, there's no such thing as a little project." Finally, it demonstrates it with the spectacular work of its teams at Mount Rushmore, on the Christ statue overlooking the Bay of Rio de Janeiro, and in Saint Peter's square in Rome.

Intentions, stakes, visions, beliefs and values

Ah, yes, those famous values…

What brand hasn't gone off in search of its values over the last twenty years? When it was changing its visual identity, Michelin's objective was to express the brand's values, in other words "innovation on behalf of the client", whence the final choice of the Michelin man "saluting," with arm raised, rather than a "go-getter, aggressive" Michelin man.

While changing its ad campaign in September 2000, Renault explained that a huge study of the brand's identity undertaken over two years had enabled it to zero in on the values that guide the company: "It is visionary, audacious, and warm."

Nivea's blue color is supposed to evoke "sympathy, harmony, loyalty, and friendship." At Kraft-Jacobs, it is declared that the central value of Hollywood chewing gum is that "happiness goes to those who dare". Quicksilver works with the notions of "authenticity, pleasure, freedom, and tribe." Gap's values are "independence and individualism." Chanel's are "modernity, insolence." Nike: "determination and victory." Absolut: "clarity, simplicity, perfection." At one time, Club Med embodied "generosity, sensuality, creativity, beauty, and friendliness," but also, in another interview, "youth, mischief, freedom, and well-being," or again, "relaxation, family gatherings, kids, action, personal growth."

Please, enough! When you can put just about anything and its opposite in the list of a brand's values, what this implies is that the word has lost much of its meaning, especially since even the best intentions mean nothing unless they are put into practice. Can you guess which brand has as its values "family, trust, solidity, accessibility, modesty, and tact"? No?[33] That's because values alone don't create identity any more than a brand's image, positioning, or territory do. The advantage of all this babble about brand "values" is that it enables us to read between the lines and to discern what brands don't always reveal: that their identity bears within it a utopia, and that many projects consist in bringing this utopia to life. If I had to cite just one example as proof, giving honor where honor is due, I would point to the famous chorus accompanying a TV spot for Coca-Cola in the early 1970s:

I'd like to buy the world a home and furnish it with love,

Grow apple trees, honey bees, and snow white turtledoves,

I'd like to teach the world to sing in perfect harmony.

A promising beginning, which is spoiled a bit by the following verses:

I'd like to buy the world a Coke and keep it company,

That's the real thing, what the world wants today,

Is the real thing.

Utopian projects

Utopias are all over the place in the world of brands, just as much as values but less visibly, such that one wonders whether utopia isn't the real foundation of brand identity.

This was clearly the case with Apple in the Steve Jobs era in any case, or with Phil Kgnight at Nike or Howard Schultz at Starbucks, two entrepreneurs who were less flamboyant but visionary in their own way. It's also the case, in a more discreet vein, with Air France, ("Making the sky the best place on earth") or Kenzo perfumes, "So that the world stays beautiful."

Some brands, however, are content to have more modest ambitions, like Philips: "Let's make things better." But halfway between the bare minimum and the utopian fantasy, there are brands whose "programs," although less extravagant, have the merit of being clear and even realistic. Patagonia, for example: "We have a specific idea of extreme sports as a means of getting closer to the wilderness. We must defend this identity." Or else Compaq, which no longer defines itself today as a computer manufacturer but as the brand that develops all information-access products: microphones, internet terminals, electronic planners, and so on. Or IBM, which offers "solutions for a small planet."

This is also the case with brands that want to become the go-to brand in their respective markets, like Decathlon, which "must become the Nokia, the Sony, the Ikea of French sports," or Babybel, which wants to become "the Coca-Cola of cheese," just as Gap wanted to be the "Coca-Cola of clothing" and Stimorol the "Absolut vodka" of chewing gum.

A final category of project invites the consumer to become part of the implicit utopia contained within the project. There are many examples, and here we once again encounter the authoritarian tendencies common to a great many brands, which I already discussed earlier:

- Lancôme: "Believe in beauty";

- Camper: "Imagine";

- Hewlett-Packard: "Invent";

- Siemens: "Be inspired";

- Lacoste: "Become what you are";

- Hugo Boss: "Don't imitate, innovate";

- Sony: "Go create."

Or, back to the bare minimum, Calvin Klein, with its CK be perfume: "Just be". Incidentally, this was also the motto of D. Packard, one of the two founders of Hewlett-Packard, a brand that was notoriously allergic to advertising and that thought, like its founding father, that it's pointless to trumpet one's values—it suffices to live them.

KEY POINTS

- The Physical Pole encompasses all of the concrete elements that make it possible to recognize a brand without any possible confusion with another brand.

- The Temporal Pole makes it possible to determine to what degree the brand uses the temporal dimension (past, present, future, timelessness) as the basis of its identity.

- The Spatial Pole works the same way, but with space instead of time. (here, there, nowhere/anywhere)

- The Norms Pole helps identify the brand's tendency to respect or violate market norms, and to determine whether that behavior is a fundamental aspect of its identity.

- The Relations Pole makes it possible to say whether a brand's use of a certain type of relations with the public (trust, proximity, seriousness, etc.) is a constant of that brand's identity.

- The Positions Pole establishes the nature of the respective positions occupied by the brand and the consumers (symmetrical or complementary).

- The Projects Pole makes it possible to determine whether the intentions of the brand (and not of the company that is its legal owner) do or do not play a role in its identity.

*   *   *

HOW TO USE THE FINGERPRINT METHOD

> Having outlined the contents of the seven Poles, the last step consists in explaining the rules of the game for applying the Fingerprint Method, and determining which players can participate.

For reasons I've already gone into, I chose to arrange the seven contexts of communication not head-to-tail in the form of a list, but rather in a geometrical figure with seven poles.

Sometimes I don't use the circle, and then I get a heptagon. But the heptagon, besides the fact that its name isn't very engaging, is a closed figure, which denatures the meaning of identity as described here—I see identity as something open, and interesting not because of what it "contains" but because of the exchange that takes place between itself and the outside, or among its seven poles. In other words, its content is less important than the system of internal or external relationships of which it is formed.

Moreover, there's a tendency to position a geometrical figure pretty much in the center of the space where it's found: for example, lined up on the page of a book. But in this case, one of the seven points of the heptagon will invariably be positioned straight up, and being on top of the others, will be given more weight and importance than the others. This would unbalance the Fingerprint Method, in which the seven poles are equidistant and arranged around a circle so that none of them is in a position of superiority with respect to the others

Even more important: the Fingerprint Method tries to break from any old mental mold and doesn't look at brand identity as if it were some venerable treasure chest or an hermetic, sealed safe. So, no closed geometrical figure would be consistent with its systemic, flexible, and fluid approach.

Thus, as satisfying for the eye and intellectually comfortable a pretty seven-pointed star may look, I choose to inscribe the heptagon inside a circle, erase the star and keep the seven points, or seven poles. Of course, this circle is not closed; it's just a dotted line along which the poles are positioned.

The order in which they are arranged around the dotted circle is random, but it also obeys a certain logic.

It's random to the extent that the Physical pole, for example, could be anywhere on the circle. And it obeys a certain logic because the Physical pole should be sandwiched between the Temporal and Spatial poles. The four others can switch positions, provided they also remain grouped together.

Why?

Because the Physical, Spatial, and Temporal poles are (relatively) more tangible than the four others, and we'll soon see why it is important to check that the brand fingerprint covers both groups, and not just one. This is more apparent if the two groups are distinct.

A VERY BRIEF USER'S MANUAL

1. Decide for what length of time (5, 10, or more years) and over which area (region, country, zone) you're going to study the brand. The longer and the wider the time and space frames are, the more difficult the exercise (you risk getting buried under an avalanche of information). It's better to do several fingerprints.

2. Collect all the information you can find about your brand, big or small, obvious or not. Do not reject anything at this point.

3. Arrange these pieces of information around the circle, on each of the relevant poles. The same information can go onto several poles (for example: Swatch can be connected to the Physical, the Norms and the Temporal poles).

4. Figure out which poles attract the most information.

5. Focus on these poles, review all the information, and now select those which are relevant for your brand only (for example: "hamburger" is not relevant enough if you are studying a fast-food brand, since several of them can claim that's what they make). Look for everything that differentiates your brand (the fewer distinguishing features, the weaker the brand's identity).

6. This should leave you with 2, 3, or 4 poles: those which have the most distinct traits.

   o Less than two poles is okay only if you're a very young brand, or a very small niche brand: it's already time to think ahead about which poles you're most likely to develop successfully in the years to come, and to begin working on them.

   o More than four poles is okay only if you're a big brand; if you are not studying a big brand, more than four poles means that you probably didn't select your information carefully enough. When in doubt, turn to the customers (yours AND those of your competitor(s)) for their opinion. If, for instance, they don't say anything that relates to the Spatial Pole, forget about it, even if you think you've done a good job and have been spending lots of money on it.

7. Draw a line to connect the selected poles: you get at the very least one line, usually three (that is, a triangle) or four (a quadrangle). That's your fingerprint, in other words, the most frequent path followed by your brand over the years Remember it's not a prison but a compass which gives you a general direction, not how to get there. The "how" is yours: that's where innovation and creativity can make a difference.

In the end, the same is true for brand identity management as it is for any management: be clear about your goals, flexible about how to reach them, not the other way round.

THE IKEA EXAMPLE

■ Physical Pole: very strong (colors, products name, products (Billy, for instance: immediately recognizable), product convenience and durability (mattresses tests); DIY assembly system; store locations and size, in-store itinerary and services; prices; catalog.

- Temporal Pole: not very strong. By default: a contemporary brand.

- Spatial Pole: very strong (Scandinavian design, Swedish brand, Swedish names, Swedish restaurants + in-store organization, often copied, never matched).

- Norms: very strong (unconventional, modern approach to furniture and lifestyle).

- Positions: strong (asymmetrical: Ikea is the creator and provider of a global concept; the client recognizes this and enjoys the brand's innovativeness, convenience and prices).

- Relations: very strong, original and complementary (lots of serious thinking and planning in the design, production and distribution processes + a sense of humor in advertising).

- Projects: less clear today than at the beginning (giving young people in devastated post-Second World War Sweden, and then Europe, access to good-quality, modern, well-designed, affordable furniture).

To sum up:

+ Four very strong poles (Physical, Spatial, Norms, Relations)

+ Two strong ones (Positions, Projects)

+ One neutral pole (Temporal)

= a very strong identity

Its quadrangular fingerprint doesn't mean that Ikea should never change it, or that three out of four poles are weak, only that when it will change (and sooner or later, since it's a living identity, it will), the brand will be able to switch from one pole to another, currently less active one (let's say, from Norms to Projects), without threatening its identity : three stable poles out of four are enough for the public to recognize the brand while understand it's evolving. What's more, each one of these three stable poles can remain active and still change, but from the inside (for instance, by switching inside the Time pole from Today to Tomorrow), so as to remain stable over time. That way, the brand can keep its identity in a dynamic balance – the same one that helps you ride a bicycle.[34]

THE RULES OF THE GAME

Understanding and guiding the evolving identity of a brand isn't the same thing as forcing it to evolve or trying to make it evolve faster: you can't make grass grow by pulling on it.

Instead, with the Fingerprint Method, it's a matter of using an observation tool that is *also* a guiding tool, a means of taking action. The action in question is organized around two main objectives:

■ Ensuring the stability of brand identity, while remaining aware that it's always a *dynamic* stability, an equilibrium *in* and *through* movement, and not a rigid attempt to cling on to existing gains or values.

■ Enabling change when change is necessary, possible, and desirable.

From these two objectives there follow the four principal rules of this subtle and exciting game, which is more like the game of go than like chess.

1) The two most common eventualities come down to choosing between a gradual and a more radical change.

   o When it's a matter of making identity change without modifying either the nature or the number of poles identified as being the most important, it's enough for the brand to move *within* each of the poles. For example within the Temporal pole, by moving from the past to the present, or from the present to the future, or by associating past and present, as Hermès did in 2011 with its "Contemporary artisan since 1837" campaign.

   o When the need arises to make the change in identity more visible, one of the identity poles can be laid to rest or sacrificed (the weakest, the hardest or most costly to maintain, or the one that's least relevant in the new context), and another chosen to replace it. Imagine that there were three key poles: if one is neutralized, two remain (and preserving two-thirds of the original identity is in itself a guarantee of continuity), *plus* four others from which a new pole is chosen. The whole is reconfigured but not thrown out of balance.

2) Most brands that are in good health work with three or four poles. Only two poles and we're dealing with a niche brand, or one that's young or ailing—three legs is the minimum to keep a stool upright. But only the most powerful brands, like Ikea or Starbucks, have the means to work with five, six, or seven poles at once: for the rest, it's neither necessary nor desirable to do this. The goal isn't to activate all the poles at

once but only those that make true differentiation, and thus identity, possible.

3) Most brands that wonder about their identity have been around for a while. A brand that is just being born might have an *intended* identity, but no established identity yet. History builds identity. And not only history: expansion in space, too. An international brand never has the same identity everywhere in the world, whatever its managers may say, and that's a good sign, the proof that the process of co-creating the brand with the consumers is working well. Where analysis is concerned, the consequence is that to take local variants and evolutions over time into account, the Fingerprint Method must be framed in time and space: for example, from 2000 to 2005 in Brazil. Before 2000 or after 2005, and in other countries, the same exercise has to be performed, and the results compared. If, for example, one obtains four slightly different fingerprints in four countries or four zones, provided they share at least two poles in common, the brand identity is sufficiently consistent.

4) Marketing isn't the only thing to have an influence on brand identity, far from it. In reality, four actors can have an impact:

   o The company that has legal ownership of the brand (a rapid or brutally sudden turnover, a change in stakeholders, or a merger can have unexpected consequences on the identity of the brands concerned).

   o The consumers, of course, act directly or indirectly on brand identity, as Gap, which was forced to withdraw its new logo after protests on Facebook and Twitter, experienced in autumn 2011. And where would Harley-Davidson be without the loyal crowd that believes in the brand and puts it to use?

   o The competition is liable to have an effect on a brand's identity. Although the French company had a long history of road mapping behind it going back to 1908, Google Maps prevented Michelin from developing its aborted ViaMichelin project on the GPS market. But sometimes, too, the competition is what sparks the emergence of a new and powerful brand identity: Apple wouldn't be Apple without IBM.

   o The fourth and final actor is perhaps the least known but also certainly the most powerful because it can act alone or in combination with the three others: chance. At Sony, Guinness, Kellogg's, or Michelin, in the life of brands and everywhere else, it reigns as the invisible and unpredictable master, except perhaps in Asian countries where every enterprise takes it into account, starting with the famous military strategies of Sun-Tzu, which we admire so much and understand so poorly.

In the West, we believe in the supreme power of the will, and not only is marketing no exception to the rule, but it takes virile posturing to the next level, promising stunning success—so long as we follow its precepts. Its maniacal rationalism leads it relentlessly to track down the causes of brand success and failure, in order to derive lessons that would make it possible to avoid the latter and to achieve the former, guaranteed. In this bazaar of fool-proof recipes, there are plenty of salesmen, except for the one who would take the risk of recalling that there is no such thing as an infallible method, and that if there exist conditions that are more likely to favor success than others, there's no way to prevent chance from rearing its head unexpectedly.

But if marketing had to recognize the role that chance plays in the life of brands, it would sabotage itself, because marketing is essentially about selling certainties, methods, examples—even, if it comes to that, in the form of twenty-two supposedly "immutable" laws.[35]

We can have only compassion for those who are taken in by the pure marketing artifice that sells them nothing but the author's talent. There are no laws in marketing, just a few rules, and thus just as many exceptions. And if I had to give just one, it would be: sooner or later, chance will come along and wreak havoc with your plans, and you won't be able to tell in advance whether it's for worse or for better.

KEY POINTS

- The Fingerprint Method produces a geometrical design (a triangle, a square, a pentagon, etc.) that links the poles most often activated by the brand over the course of a long period of time (at least five to ten years).

- This design represents the brand's identity and serves as a guide for action when questions of identity are raised.

- It must be traced within a specific spatial and temporal frame, with several tracings corresponding to several stages in the brand's life.

- Four actors participate, willingly or not, in the creation and evolution of brand identity: the company with legal ownership of the brand, the public, the competitors, and chance.

CONCLUSION

Finally, and to get back to the question that many think is the most important one: what is brand identity's purpose?

First, to make money. The professionals all say so, including the most pragmatic among them, like Sergio Zyman.

For thirteen years, at two different periods, he was the head of marketing at Coca-Cola, and the least that can be said of him is that he's neither a dreamer nor a softy. The photo on the cover of his book[1] leaves no doubt about it, nor does the nickname the American advertising gurus gave him: they called him the Aya-cola. His conception of marketing is radical enough to horrify his most orthodox peers, but at the same time, he doesn't shrink from overturning their most deeply rooted convictions. In addition to Coke, he was also responsible for Fanta, and he tells how every time he wanted to increase sales, the solution was to launch new varieties (apple, raspberry, and so on), with some very disturbing results. Why disturbing? Because Fanta was originally a lemon-based drink, and the new flavors were diluting the integrity of the brand's identity. Even though sales kept increasing, the brand was going to lose out in the long run, because its identity was deteriorating. "If we had continued that way," he writes, "we would have stopped making any money at all."

Brand identity also serves to conquer markets. The president of Shiseido wants to become the leader in the cosmetics sector in the twenty-first century. Asked how he would do this, he replied:

> We're trying to highlight the identity of Shiseido, which was founded in the Ginza district in Tokyo. In a globalizing world, it's very important for a company to preserve its identity. It's by respecting that identity that we'll be able to go international and achieve our goals.[2]

Absolut Vodka has demonstrated the point: only a strong identity made it possible for the brand to penetrate the very closed vodka market in the United States, and we know how carefully this identity was fashioned, maintained, and protected. Cadbury also thinks that its identity is what facilitated its international expansion.[3]

Finally, brand identity keeps brands alive, and the clearer the identity, the longer the life of the brand. At Ikea, the brand's identity is so limpid and so crucial that it's the first of the "nine commandments" decreed by founder Ingvar Kamprad ("No. 1: product range—our identity. Large range of designed and functional products at low prices").

Conversely, what happens when a brand doesn't have a strong identity?

It has trouble conquering new markets, as the CEO of Wal-Mart Europe acknowledged. With flagships established in Britain and Germany, and less than 350 stores in various formats, he was asked whether he foresaw making further acquisitions in order to reach critical mass in other European countries. What did he reply?

> The problem isn't the size, but the identity of the brand. In both the food and the non-food sectors, we have as much purchasing power as any big European distributor. We want to be the best, not the biggest.

This project must not have been based on a sufficiently strong identity, because Wal-Mart threw in the towel and left Europe in 2006.

* * *

Identity has become a key concept in marketing that no brand today can do without. The brands that have an identity protect and watch over it carefully, and the rest wonder what they can do to get one, or how to strengthen or manage the one they have. There isn´t a single problem—mergers, acquisitions, diversifications, relational marketing, advertising, sponsoring, gift-giving, promotion, social-networking, etc.—that doesn't have something to do, in some way or another, with the question of brand identity. Directors and commentators bears witness to this fact with each interview they give: "Identity is a company´s most valuable asset,"[4] it is "central for the brand's strategic vision."[5] Identity is even becoming an integral part of the definition of a brand, as could be seen at the entrance to an exhibition in London on the subject in January 2001. The first sign that welcomed visitors stated:

> A brand is a name or a symbol that sets a product or a service apart from its competitors. In today's business world, each brand is endowed with a complex identity created by marketing, advertising, public relations, and designers. The value of a brand is based on the public's acceptance of this identity.[6]

And for those who were wondering what the secret of the biggest brands is, the answer is the same:

> Brand identity was the cornerstone of Coca-Cola´s strategy.[7]

Once everyone is in agreement about the importance of brand identity, it remains to examine how marketing conceives this central concept. The truth is that it conceives brand identity today in exactly the same way as, in days gone by, it conceived most of its "concepts": by applying to brands ideas from another age. These ideas are, it is true, venerable ones, but they are also more and more out of sync with an era that is in the process of radically redefining concepts such as identity.

The proof? It can be found by comparing what was said about identity yesterday and what is being said about it today.

A good illustration of the way in which identity was traditionally understood is offered by one of the world´s most eminent biologists, winner of the Nobel Prize for Medicine in 1965, François Jacob. In *The Statue Within*, his memoirs, he begins by asking the inevitable question: "How did I end up becoming who I am?" And this is how he responds: ¨I carry within me, sculpted since childhood, a sort of interior statue that lends continuity to my life and that is the most intimate part of me, the most solid core of my character. I have sculpted that statue all my life."[8]

When Jacob says "since childhood," he means since the 1920s. His testimony is invaluable, but it dates from a past that keeps on receding as more and more water flows under the bridge. The conditions of life have changed, mentalities have evolved. It's not so much a matter of knowing whether this evolution is good or bad as of figuring out where we're heading. And all the signs point to increasing dilution. The "solid core" that was supposed to contain and protect individual identity in its most concentrated essence is in the process of dissolving. As a result, brand identity can no longer be understood as an extension of human identity without taking this dissolving process into account. It is more and more often the case that the statue within has become a mere sand sculpture.

The reasons for this shift are many and well known. Sociologists can't stop reminding us of them: redefinition of the borders between male and female identities, breaking up of the traditional family structure, reshaping of the social landscape due to the mixing effects of immigration, loss of ideological reference points such as religious and political affiliations, multifaceted and redefined professional identities—in short, none of the great fixed points around which former generations defined themselves remain any longer. We have entered the era of the "uncertain individual,"[9] of a generalized "identity crisis,"[10] and the secret reveries of a bygone childhood are no longer ours. Instead, we are left with the insights of Brecht when he said that our permanence is made up exclusively of changes, and that our body doesn't have the relative stability that we believe it possesses, but instead is an abstract structure animated by a flux of material that adapts to a slowly evolving form.

Can a discipline like marketing, which wants to place itself at the cutting edge of modernity, afford to be unaware of these transformations? The answer, obviously, is no. That is why this book was conceived as a machine for wiping out received ideas (including my own) about brand identity. The exercise is a risky one, but it is impossible to sit back and watch such a radical evolution in our conception of identity without drawing the consequences for applications in other fields of human experience— marketing, for example. We have to choose between two solutions: either we dig in our heels and cling to our old ways of thinking, or else we try to assist in the emergence of a new approach to identity, and to draw the conclusions that follow when this concept is applied to brands.

I have chosen the second solution, and I invite all people who work in the world of marketing and brands to do the same.

And if I had to give just one reason for them to do so, I would offer this one: the life of brands is changing so fast that we can no longer be content with an overly static conception of identity. I don't mean that we should go too far in the opposite direction and behave like a weathervane without taking into account any of the lessons of the past. I merely believe that these lessons should not be transformed into a kind of ball and chain that holds us back. Inheritances that are too heavy to carry lead their benefactors to ruin more often than to prosperity.

By speaking of a brand's "genetic code," by presenting identity as immovable, untouchable, and practically sacred, classical marketing constructed a taboo that speaks eloquently about its own superstitions but does few favors to companies facing the problems posed by the evolution of brands. We can't tell them both: "Make radical changes" and "Don't touch brand identity." The slightest change has incalculable consequences for brand identity because there is no such thing as, on the one hand, a "surface" on which various modifications take place, and on the other the "depths" where nothing ever moves and where identity makes its home. This distinction is fallacious, as everyone now realizes. Nor can we tell them: "Don't enter that market" or "Change your pricing" for the sole reason that their identity forbids or permits such a step: if moving to a new market or changing prices is the only solution to a given problem, it would be stupid to give it up. If the brand is solid, its identity will survive, provided one takes a bare minimum of precautions. Otherwise, defending its identity will be of little help in any event.

No, it is better to rethink brand identity, to release it from the rigid framework in which it has been locked up, and to make it evolve in the same direction as identity itself. But in order to do this, we must agree to give up our intellectual crutches.

Just yesterday, the identity concept seemed so clear and solid. Today, if one consults with the specialists, it isn't either anymore. Of course, one can always pretend that nothing has changed. There are people who keep walking straight ahead even in the void—it's a well-known joke in the cartoons.

Or else we can set off on the adventure of a new way of thinking, doing our best to take the most recent information and research into account.

This isn't the easiest way, but it is the most interesting, and in the long term, the most useful one for brands.

NOTES

INTRODUCTION

1. Naomi Klein, *No Logo: Taking Aim at Brand Bullies*, Knopf, 2000.
2. Guy Deutscher, *Through the Language Glass: Why the World Looks Different in Other languages*, Random House, 2010.
3. Also called Palo Alto School or Invisible College, initially a group of researchers working at the Mental Research Institute in Palo Alto, California, in the 50s and 60s, including G. Bateson, P. Watzlawick, D. Jackson, and M. H. Erickson.
4. See J. Gerzema and E. Lebar, *The Brand Bubble, The Looming Crisis in Brand Value and How to Avoid it*, Jossey-Bass, 2008.
5. Brands are in reality as old as commercial exchange, and traces of them are found in numerous archeological sites around the Mediterranean, some dating from several millennia BC., in the form of seal-cylinders. The oldest brand whose name has survived to date is Fortis, a brand of tiles used in the construction of numerous Roman villas around the year 100 BC.
6. L. B. Upshaw, *Building Brand Identity*, Wiley & Sons, 1995.
7. D. Schultz and H. Schultz, *Brand Babble: Sense and Nonsense about Branding*, South-Western Educational Pub, 2003.
8. We owe the expression "new communication" to John H. Weakland (*Communication and Behavior, An Introduction*, introduction to the special issue of the *American Behavioral Scientist* devoted to communication and edited by John H. Weakland, 1967).
9. P. Watzlawick, J. H. Beavin, Don D. Jackson, *Pragmatics of Human Communication: A Study of Interactional Patterns, Pathologies and Paradoxes*, WW Norton & Co, 1967.
10. A. Damasio, *The Feeling of What Happens: Body and Emotion in the Making of Consciousness*, Mariner, 2000.

I   A PARADOXICAL SUCCESS STORY

1. Z. Bauman, *Identity*, Polity Press, 2006.
2. C. Lévi-Strauss, *L'Identité*, Presses Universitaires de France, 2007.
3. L. B. Upshaw, *Building Brand Identity*, Wiley & Sons, 1995.
4. H. Maucher, *Leadership in Action*, McGraw-Hill, 1994 (the French title was: *La Stratégie Nestlé: principles simples pour diriger dans un monde complexe* (Maxima, 2005), which translates as *The Nestlé Strategy: Simple Principles for Leadership in a Complex World*.
5. *Harvard Business Review*, "Embracing Complexity," September 2011.
6. *Financial Times, Les Échos*, Pricewaterhouse Coopers, *L'art du marketing*, Village Mondial, 2000.
7. A. Ries and J. Trout, Harper Business, 1994.
8. A. Ries and L. Ries, Harper Business, 2002.
9. J. Vee, T. Miller, and J. Bauer, Wiley, 2008.
10. See the very title of the journal *Marketing Science*.

11. Among the most recent examples: *The Darwin Economy: Liberty, Competition, and the Common Good*, Robert H. Frank, Princeton University Press, 2011.

12. A. Ries and L. Ries, *The Origin of Brands: Discover the Natural Laws of Product Innovation and Business Survival*, Collins, 2004.

13. Darwin, *The Origin of Species*.

14. "The concept of brand image, that I made popular in 1953, wasn't truly new. C. Hopkins had described it twenty years earlier." D. Ogilvy, *On Advertising*, Vintage Books, 1985.

15. D. A. Aaker, *Building Strong Brands*, Simon & Schuster Ltd., 2002.

16. J.-N. Kapferer, *Strategic Brand Management*, Kogan Page, 1997.

17. *Full House: The Spread of Excellence from Plato to Darwin,* Harmony Books, 1996

18. Free Press, 1991.

19. Free Press, 1995.

20. Upshaw, *Building Brand Identity*.

21. R. S. Tedlow, *The Rise and Fall of Mass Marketing*, Van Nostrand Reinhold, 1993.

22. Richard Tedlow, *The Story of Mass-Marketing in America,* Harvard Business School Press, 1996.

23. S. Bedbury, *A Brand New World*, Penguin Books, 2003.

24. N. Kochan, *The World's Greatest Brands,* New York University Press, 1997.

25. *The World's Greatest Brands.*

26. D. E. Carter, *Branding: The Power of Market Identity*, Wapson-Guptill Publications, 1999.

27. Only in retrospect did semiologists suggest a link with the initial "Mother" or "Mummy", just as they suggested one between hamburger, hot, soft, elastic, with the maternal breast. Two powerful symbolic attributes for a food brand.

28. F. Gilmore, *Brand Warriors: Corporate Leaders Share their Winning Strategies*, HarperCollins Business, 1997.

29. A. Perry and D. Wisnom, *Before the Brand: Creating the Unique DNA of an Enduring Brand Identity*, McGraw-Hill, 2003.

30. Upshaw, *Building Brand Identity*.

31. Kapferer, *Strategic Brand Management.*

2   WHAT'S THE STATE OF AFFAIRS TODAY?

1. 1950, to be exact, the year in which E. Erikson introduced the concept in the humanities with his book *Childhood and Society*, W.W. Norton & Co., 1993.

2. Richard Tedlow, *The Story of Mass-Marketing in America,* Harvard Business School Press, 1996.

3. Upshaw, *Building Brand Identity, op. cit.*

4. Aaker, *Building Strong Brands*

5. P. Kotler, *Marketing Management*.

6. Kapferer, *Strategic Brand Management, op. cit.*

7. *Cybernetics, or the Control and Communication in the Animal and the Machine*, MIT Press, 1965.

8. S. Kamakau (1815–76), *Tales and Traditions of the People of Old*, Bishop Museum Press, 1993.

9. See the work of S. Moscovici or W. Wagner and N. Hayes, *Everyday Discourse and Common Sense: the Theory of Social Representation*, Palgrave Macmillan, 2005.

10. M.-C. Sicard, *La métamorphose des Marques*, Editions d'Organisation, Paris, 1998.

11. To borrow A. Toffler's terminology in *Future Shock¸* Bantam, 1984.

12. D. Lynch and P. Kordis, *The Strategy of the Dolphin*, William Morrow & Co., 1989.

13. G. L. Decker, *Winning with the P&G 99*, Pocket Books, 1998.
14. In other words, they go back to 1837.
15. J. C. Collins and J. I. Porras, *Harper Business*, 1997.
16. J. Séguéla, *Hollywood lave plus blanc*, Flammarion, 1992.
17. G. Debord, *The Society of the Spectacle*, Black and Red; Reprint, 2010 edition (first appeared in French in 1967).
18. *Hollywood lave plus blanc.*
19. *Hollywood lave plus blanc.*
20. Edgar Morin, *The Stars*, Grove Press, 1961.
21. G. Lipovetsky, *L'Ère du vide*, Gallimard, 1989.
22. M. Maffesoli, *The Time of the Tribe*, Sage Publications Ltd, 1996.
23. A. Maalouf, *In the Name of Identity: Violence and the Need to Belong*, Arcade Publishing, 2001.
24. A. Ries and J. Trout, *Marketing Warfare*, McGraw Hill, 1985.
25. A. Maalouf, *op. cit.*
26. For examples, see the following: L. B. Upshaw, *Building Brand Identity*, Wiley & Sons, 1995; D. A. Aaker, *Building Strong Brands*, Simon & Schuster Ltd, 2002; L. de Chernatony and M. McDonald, *Creating Powerful Brands*, Butterworth Heinemann, 1998; D. Arnold, *The Handbook of Brand Management*, Perseus, 1993; G. Michel, *La Stratégie d'extension de marque*, Vuibert, 2000; B. Schmitt, A. Simonson, *Marketing Aesthetics*, Free Press, 1997.
27. Kapferer, *op. cit.*
28. *Strategic Brand Management.*
29. *Building Strong Brands.*
30. *Le Marketing de la marque, op. cit.*
31. S. Randazzo, *Mythmaking on Madison Avenue*, Probus Pub. Co, 1993.
32. J-P. Sartre, *Being and Nothingness [L'Etre et le Néant]*, Gallimard, 1943.
33. *Propaganda*, the first handbook of public relations and manipulation of public opinion was published in 1928 by Edward Bernays, a nephew of Freud.

3   REDEFINING BRAND IDENTITY

1. *La Marque, op. cit.*
2. *La Métamorphose des Marques, op. cit.*
3. "Karl Popper, the great philosopher of science, once divided the world into two categories: clocks and clouds. Clocks are neat, orderly systems that can be solved through reduction; clouds are an epistemic mess, 'highly irregular, disorderly, and more or less unpredictable.' The mistake of modern science is to pretend that everything is a clock, which is why we get seduced again and again by the false promises of brain scanners and gene sequencers. We want to believe we will understand nature if we find the exact right tool to cut its joints. But that approach is doomed to failure. We live in a universe not of clocks but of clouds." J. Lehrer, author of *Proust was a Neuroscientist*, Mifflin Harcourt, 2007, in scienceblog.com, June 2010.
4. E. Morin, *Penser l'Europe*, Gallimard, 1990.
5. Ibid.
6. F. Varela, *The Embodied Mind: Cognitive Science and Human Experience*, The MIT Press, new edition, 1993.
7. *The Feeling of What Happens: Body and Emotions in the Making of Consciousness*, Mariner Books, 2000.
8. J.-M. Lévy Leblond, *Aux contraires*, Gallimard, 1996.

9. P. Mannoni, *Les Représentations sociales,* coll. "Que sais-je?", Presses Universitaires de France, 2006.
10. *Understanding Brands,* Kogan Page, 2006.
11. P. Mannoni.
12. Ibid.
13. E. Morin, *Pour sortir du XXe siècle,* Le Seuil, 1984.
14. H. Atlan, *Entre le cristal et la fumée, essai sur l'organisation du vivant,* Le Seuil, 1986.
15. G. Balandier, *Le Désordre,* Fayard, 1998.
16. A. Danchin and A. Quayle, *The Delphic Boat,* Harvard University Press, 2003.
17. Penguin, 2005.
18. *The Feeling of What Happens.*
19. Nobel Prize in Medicine, 1965.
20. *The Statue Within,* Cold Spring Harbor Laboratory Press, 1995.
21. *Scientific American,* March 1998.

4   THE FINGERPRINT METHOD CONCEPT

1. In French, the word *marque* could mean any of the following: a brand, a mark, a trace, or an imprint.
2. G. Miller, *The Psychological Review,* 1956, vol. 63, 81–97.
3. H. Gardner, *The Mind's New Science: a History of the Cognitive Revolution,* Basic Books, 1987.
4. A. Mucchielli, *Les sciences de l'information et de la communication,* 4th edition, Hachette Supérieur, 2006.
5. D. de Kerckhove, *Skin of Culture,* Kogan Page, 1998.
6. P. Breton and D. Bade, *The Culture of the Internet, and the Internet as a Cult,* Litwin Books, LLC, 2011.
7. P. Watzlawick, *The Language of Chance,* W. W. Norton Co., 1993.
8. Mail-order European leader.
9. M. Batey, *Brand Meaning,* Psychology Press, 2008, or A. Arvidsson, *Brands, Meaning, and Value in Media Culture,* Routledge, 2006.
10. Among others: R. Rose, J. Pulizzi, *Managing Content Marketing: the Real-World Guide for Creating Passionate Subscribers to Your Brand,* CMI Books, 2011.
11. P. Watzlawick (dir.), *The Invented Reality, Contributions to Constructivism,* W. W. Norton & Co., 1980.

5   THE FINGERPRINT METHOD: THE SEVEN POLES

1. *Brand Warriors, op. cit.*
2. T. Levitt, "Marketing Myopia", *Harvard Business Review,* 1960.
3. Interbrand ranking, 2011.
4. "Without touch, we can't connect. Without skin, we can't touch."
5. "Is gentle something you touch, or something that touches you?"
6. Another (feminine) perfume by Cacharel.
7. The snaps were recently replaced with classic buttons, easy to sew back on if need be, and just like the ones that all the other brands use.

8. *Brand Warriors, op. cit.*
9. *L'Entreprise,* October 1998.
10. Catalogue of the "Brand New" exhibit, London, Victoria & Albert Museum, 2000.
11. *Guerilla Advertising,* Lawrence King Publishing, 2006.
12. It's 2008 ad campaign slogan: "Happiness wasn't born in Brazil, it's a naturalized citizen."
13. M. Halter, *Shopping for Identity,* Schocken Books, 2000.
14. B. H. Schmitt, *Experiential Marketing, How to Get Customers to Sense, Feel, Think, Act, and Relate to Your Company and Brands,* Free Press, 1999.
15. Pernod-Ricard, the world's second biggest manufacturer and distributer of wines and spirits.
16. D. Sperber, *La Contagion des idées,* Odile Jacob, 1996.
17. *Brand Warriors, op. cit.*
18. *Fortune,* July 1999.
19. Mellerio dit Meller, as we have seen, disputes this.
20. J. Séguéla, *Pub Story,* Hoëbeck, 1992.
21. *Le Nouvel Observateur,* April 2007.
22. *Doing Cultural Studies: The Story of the Sony Walkman,* Sage Publications, 1997.
23. A. Swasy, *Soap Opera, the Inside Story of Procter & Gamble,* Times Books, Random House, 1993.
24. P. Watzlawick and J. H. Weakland, *Sur l'interaction,* Le Seuil, 2004.
25. James H. and Gilmore, B. Joseph Pine II, *Authenticity,* Harvard Business School Press, 2007.
26. T. Carr in *The Future of Brands,* New York University Press, 2000.
27. K. Roberts, *Lovemarks,* PowerHouse Books, 2005.
28. An advertisement from 1900, in *Cosmétiques: être et paraître,* Ghozland, 1987.
29. From a well-known series of French advertisements for the company.
30. R. Jensen, *The Dream Society,* McGraw-Hill, 2001.
31. *The Sources of the Self: The Making of Modern Identity,* Harvard University Press, 1992.
32. G. and S. Trigano, *La Saga du Club,* Grasset, 1998.
33. It's Ford.
34. This is free of charge for Ikea, a company I never worked for.
35. *The 22 Immutable Laws of Marketing, op. cit.*

CONCLUSION

1. *The End of Marketing as We Know It, op. cit.*
2. *Les Echos,* November 2000.
3. *Brand Warriors, op. cit.*
4. *Les Echos,* 28 Juin, 2000
5. *Building Strong Brands.*
6. J. Pavitt, *Brand New, op. cit.*
7. *The Story of Mass-marketing in America,* Basic Books, 1990.
8. F. Jacob, *The Statue Within,* Odile Jacob, 1996
9. A. Ehrenberg, *L'individu incertain,* Hachette Littérature, 1999.
10. C. Dubar, *La Crise des identities,* PUF, 2004.

INDEX